WHAT A FINE MESS!

Clement and Heather

Best Regards

enye!

Dan Coleman

2012

WHAT A FINE MESS!

Responding to the Economic Chaos of Government

Daniel R. Coleman, D.B.A.

Tate Publishing & Enterprises

The opinions expressed by the author are not necessarily those of Tate Publishing, LLC.

Published by Tate Publishing & Enterprises, LLC
127 E. Trade Center Terrace | Mustang, Oklahoma 73064 USA
1.888.361.9473 | www.tatepublishing.com

Tate Publishing is committed to excellence in the publishing industry. The company reflects the philosophy established by the founders, based on Psalm 68:11,
"The Lord gave the word and great was the company of those who published it."

Book design copyright © 2010 by Tate Publishing, LLC. All rights reserved.
Cover and Interior design by Blake Brasor

Published in the United States of America

ISBN: 978-1-61663-294-6
1. Political Science, Economic Conditions
2. Business & Economics, Government & Business
11.08.25

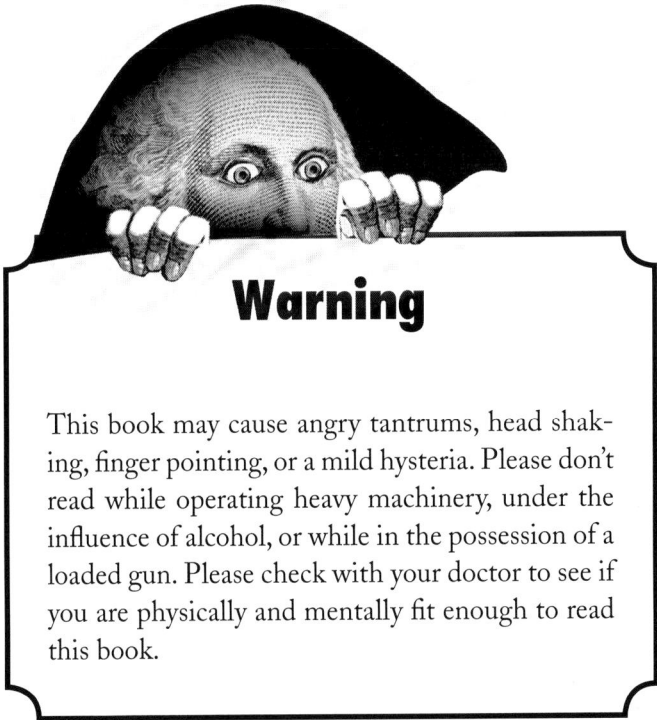

Warning

This book may cause angry tantrums, head shaking, finger pointing, or a mild hysteria. Please don't read while operating heavy machinery, under the influence of alcohol, or while in the possession of a loaded gun. Please check with your doctor to see if you are physically and mentally fit enough to read this book.

Acknowledgements

Without my faith in Christ, I would be a lost soul.

This book is dedicated to my wife, kids, and family. May it in some way help our country return to its roots.

Tamara Coleman, my wife and partner of twenty-four years. What more can be said of her patience and dedication? A constant source of encouragement and enthusiasm, she can see the positive side of any situation; and her zest for life is infectious.

Sam and Katherine Coleman, my children. These two are my pride and joy. May they always do their best in everything they attempt and know that I love them both more than I can express.

Dr. Larry Coleman, my father, professor emeritus and former chair of the Department of Insurance, College of Business, Indiana State University. He retired after thirty years of serving college students, developing relationships with industries, and developing innovative programs. He continues to serve as a role model to thousands of students as well as his own three children. Larry was an only child in a single parent family. His mother was an elementary teacher that supported her son with all her means and lived a vibrant life despite the economic hardships. Larry paid for his education while working and providing for his family. He has been a confidante, encourager, and mentor to me throughout my life and during this writing process.

Carroll Coleman, my mother, retired after devoting forty years of her life to instruction and guidance. Carroll served as an encourager for all of her students. Full of genuine and unconditional love, Carroll has served as an inspirational role model for thousands of students and especially her three children. She was one of six children whose family lived through the Great Depression. Her father was a railroad employee that saw that their needs were provided. Married at an early age, she paid to educate herself and provided a home for her children. She has always seen the best in me, even when most would have given up. Unwavering devotion to her children and husband will be her legacy.

Debra Coleman Cordell, my sister. A constant source of enthusiasm and encouragement, Deb has been eager to assist in any way possible. Unselfish to a fault, Deb has a teacher's heart and a discerning soul. Bright and vivacious, she is truly a gem.

David D. Coleman, my brother. Brother Dave, I would trust him with my life. He is the most honest, trustworthy, and forthright man I can imagine. He has garnered the respect of friends and foes alike with his selfless dedication and drive. His willingness to help others, regardless of the burden, is remarkable and serves as a shining light to others.

Author's Note

Standing in front of sixty people from various locations around the United States and the world, having just begun what would be a four-hour "hash out" international sales meeting, I realized that I was getting paid to entertain—no notes, no lectern. I was a stand-up comic in a business suit. I was being paid to be an outside facilitator; but to do that, I had to entertain. I was the entertainment.

I was given the opportunity because one of my college students was impressed or amused with my lecture style. I do have a relaxed, open, free-wheeling, and "no holds barred" style of delivery. If the students are laughing and learning, then I am quite happy. I have been teaching college classes since 1991—a little bit of management, quite a bit of marketing, but mostly economics, the dismal science. When I first started teaching, I looked young enough that I could take a classroom seat and no one knew I was the teacher. I would listen in on a conversation with those who had arrived early. (Those are usually the really good students.) Most of the time, the conversation included a discussion of what they had heard about the presiding professor and how hard the class was. I minded my own business, but I was definitely listening. As students filled in, some began to check their watches, wondering whether the instructor was going to show on time. Finally, I would stand up and say, "Well, if no one else is going to teach, I guess I will." Some thought I was joking. Others were trying to remember if they had said anything negative about their new professor.

I absolutely love to teach, and I want learning to be fun and practical. So it should not be a surprise to anyone that has taken one of my classes that I am writing under the moniker of the Economic Comic, suggested by one of my former students. All that I write about is true in my mind, but I will readily agree that I am an idealist one moment and a pragmatist the next. I am generally an optimist but can occasionally fall into the role of cynic. I am always a fiscal conservative. Some of what I believe is considered downright uncaring and mean-spirited. However, having suffered through years of "child abuse" (my parents made me work around the house and would, if needed, use a belt—neither my mom nor dad spared the rod), the case is just the opposite. I understand that short-term pain often leads to long-term avoidance of misery.

This book intends to offer an understandable view of the economic effect and impact of government on the free market. Using easy-to-remember principles, *What a Fine Mess* introduces important variations of opportunity cost, crowding out and market displacement to explain the full impact of government on the free economy in easy-to-understand language. The fundamental concepts introduced—production deficit, public efficiency contribution, market distortion, minimally acceptable production recovery, and bureaucratic value loss—offer a clearer view of the inherent challenges of involving government in economic activities. Mainstream issues such as market failure, inflation, unemployment, self-reliance, mortgage crisis, health care, welfare, international trade, and national debt round out the Economic Comic's offering. Opponents called Reagan's economic policies "voo doo" economics. I am here to tell you about "doo doo" economics.

I am sure that this book will be written off as one crazy man's version of the truth or dismissed because of my lack of economic pedigree. From one perspective it is crazy to think that this book could be some spark that leads to a powder keg of reaction. This foolhardy hope that one voice can make a difference may be my life's windmill, but it has to be said. Onward Rocinante!

Table of Contents

Introduction

One of the best books I have ever taught from was *Macro-economics*, written by Greg Mankiw. A Harvard professor and one-time member of George W. Bush's (a.k.a. Bush 43 or "W"), the 43rd president of the United States, economic team, Mankiw developed his economic text around ten basic economic principles. Why the school used it only for one year is a mystery to me. Maybe his approach confused those who counted on a traditional text.

Mankiw served as chairman of the Council of Economic Advisors for two years and then headed back to Harvard. I thought that he probably became disillusioned with a president who ran under the banner of fiscal conservatism and then changed stripes to become a binge shopper. However, Mankiw informed me that Harvard allowed for a two-year absence. He served his term and returned to teaching.

Honestly, I have never felt as betrayed as I did during Bush 43's second term. Now that I think back, maybe the elder Bush (George H.W. Bush, the 41st U.S. president, a.k.a. Bush 41), reneging on his tax promise, evoked the same type of disappointment. You think about Bush 43 and you just have to shake your head. He appeared to be a true fiscal conservative when he was the governor of

Texas. But "W" succumbed quickly to the DC disease, racking up record deficits and sending the U.S. national debt toward the ten trillion-dollar mark. The DC disease stands for "demigod confusion." What a disappointment. Instead of reducing the size of government, Bush 43 brought it to a never-seen-before rate of growth. "To infinity and beyond" must have been the thinking that almost doubled the debt in eight years.

Maybe history will be kind to W for his stand on terrorism. Suskind's portrayal of Bush in *The One Percent Doctrine* (2006) may have been an attempt at a hatchet job on Bush and Cheney, but it actually helped me understand something that I had resented. To his credit, Bush sure seemed to persevere even in the face of plummeting polls. I am going to call it courage on the terrorism front and cowardice on the fiscal policy. However, we must consider that the spending that Bush 43 allowed and the debt that was racked up has become a weakness that evildoers may exploit. By being financially irresponsible, the very situation he was trying to prevent is perpetuated by our fiscal weakness. Look at the rise of Hitler in Germany. When economic times get really tough, people will latch on to almost any idea in the hope that things will get better. It is also possible that enemies around the world may also interpret our financial weakness as an opportunity to strike at the United States.

I still use Mankiw's basic principle idea to teach economics. Of course, I modified and added to it; but it is only fair that I give credit where credit is due. The list in part one of this book is not cut into stone tablets. I have added principles and taken a few away over the years. Usually, this happens after a student asks a lucid question or makes a statement that causes convulsions. For example, when someone says, "Let's look at France to see how they are doing it," or something like, "Having health insurance should be a constitutional right of all Americans," or "Education is a basic right of every American." These naïve and well-intentioned people often set me off to devise a new principle. More often than not, it is a politician who makes some statement that no one seems to challenge, yet I find outrageous, that warrants a new principle. When President Barack Obama said, "No one is in disagreement about the need for government to act on correcting this economy," I about choked trying to disagree with the new president through the television. "No one disagrees? No one disagrees!" It is like an 800-pound man riding a tired stallion and sagely saying that everyone agrees we have to do something to make this horse run faster. I suppose that in one way Obama is correct; that is, if he means the government needs to get off the horse, or at least go on a diet. It is disheartening to me when I observe that so many people seem to accept President Obama's proclamation without question and believe the solution will come from the government. In my mind, most of our economic and many of our social problems have their roots in misguided fiscal policy. Do we want the government correcting the economy? Well, if the barn is burning, don't ask the arsonist how to put out the fire. His answer will be more matches.

With every piece of legislation, government takeover, or bailout, we are marching toward the precipice of socialism. Do you have a definition for socialism? Here's one: it is when the government owns or controls the majority of productive resources directly or through legislation. Steadily the U.S. federal government has taken on a greater role in the major industries (transportation, financial, manufacturing, health, communications, education) and increasingly regulated the four basic economic resources (land, labor, capital, and entrepreneurial talent). Those "radicals" that wrote that little document called the Constitution would likely be appalled at how easily the system, which required so much effort to create, has been so easily dispatched. Have we stopped teaching our children the sacrifice that was made by the fifty-six signers of the Constitution and lives that were lost in order to create the foundation of the freedom that we are so methodically giving away? It is absolutely amazing to me that as the rest of the world races toward free markets, the United States is lumbering toward more and more government intervention in the market, a recipe that has failed so miserably before. For those that react to crisis with the call for more regulation and more restrictions, I would propose that you: ask not what your government can do for you, ask what you will be able to do once you have allowed government to do for you.

It is not without hope that I offer up this observation called *What a Fine Mess*. I am writing this book in an effort to sound the alarm, raise the flag, and shout the warning. Hopefully the Economic Comic will be the modern day Paul Revere. Aggregately the United States is moving from self-reliance to dependence and from industriousness to entitlement. I do realize that this is not a new message, just a different horse and rider. But maybe, just maybe, this is the one strike of the stone mason that cracks the boulder that has remained impervious to earlier efforts.

PART ONE

IF I'M LYING, I'M DYING

Ten Principles on How the Government Affects the Economy

In the following pages I have offered some basic principles about the impact of government on economy that I hope will expand the conversation and lead to a new rationale when making the decision about public endeavors. This is an economic book that tries to convey the impact of our choice to use government to achieve economic or social goals. The principles are broad in scope, but each is designed to be an easy reminder of basic truths that can guide future decision making by individuals or organizations.

1

Government is inherently inefficient.

Well there's a shocker! You're really starting off with some deep stuff! Truth is, this statement is more than the usual lamentation about government waste. This goes beyond the thousand-dollar trash cans,[1] three hundred thousand-dollar public toilets,[2] or billion-dollar projects. [3] I put this principle at the very beginning because it must be figuratively drilled into the minds of Americans, because if we just look at the labor resource alone, this principle conservatively adds up to an inefficiency that represents a 1.56 trillion-dollar deficit that must be accounted for when choosing a public option, regardless of its intent or purpose.

To clarify this point, start with the idea that government basically collects money through taxes, keeps a portion for itself, and hands what is left over to someone else. Sometimes the government sends that money to people who do nothing productive for the payment. That is a problem in and of itself, but it still does not address the concept of the inherent inefficiencies of the

---

1 http://www.theworldlink.com/articles/2008/05/10/news/
doc482491801fc0f314640227.txt

2 In Pershing Square, Los Angeles, seven "automated" public toilets were installed at a cost of $300,000 each. The toilets ask passerby in several different languages to pay 25 cents and give them a try. Unfortunately, only one toilet is still running. Six nonfunctional toilets equal a cost to taxpayers of $1.8 million, not counting maintenance and upkeep from the three city departments tasked with keeping them functioning.

3 http://www.heritage.org/Research/Budget/wm839-list.cfm

public choice. Sometimes government spends the money on goods and services. This presents an issue as well, but not the one we are currently addressing. We could also examine whether government activities are wasteful or useless, but the real meaning lies deeper in the inherent nature of government.

The issue is that the "economic pie" is shortchanged when private industry employees (or other economic resources) are removed from the production process. Once removed from the private sector, the government employee no longer produces a good or service that adds to the overall private industry economic pie. As soon as a worker (or land, capital, or entrepreneurial talent) is removed from private industry, a "production deficit" is created. This is not to say that government employees are not working hard or any other vilifying notion. It simply states the fact that when you remove a worker from the production process, the economic pie is shortchanged. This expands the idea of opportunity cost—though an alternative use is part of the decision. Prior discussions of opportunity cost include the concept of using a resource here or using it there for some productive activity. Or typically, opportunity cost was used to describe consumer choice or explain the implication of business decisions when allocating scarce productive resources. Because one activity precluded the other, a choice was involved, and whatever choice you made cost you the opportunity to enjoy the other activity. Here, I impart the idea that with the "public choice" the resource is actually removed from the private industry production process; thus, instead of an opportunity cost, it is better described as a production loss. Said differently, using private industry resources for public use is not the same as simply using a resource for one purpose or the other. The production of government workers does not directly expand production in the private market; thus, a production deficit is created.

James Buchanan, Nobel Prize winner, wrote that there was a hitch with measuring the opportunity cost of "preclusionary" events. Not here, because we are not really talking about reallocation of a resource but removal. And when you remove a resource from the private sector, that loss of production is measurable. There are substantial studies that show the impact of increasing the size of government and its negative effect on economic growth. Crowding out, corruption, and operational inefficiencies of government are often blamed. A point that is often overlooked is the simple notion of the production deficit created when you choose any public endeavor.

To illustrate this point, I give you this simple example: Imagine an economy has ten workers producing 1000 units of private industry products or services. If you remove one worker, that production would drop to 900 hundred units. The worker that leaves is still working, but the resources left behind would now have to produce at least 110 units each just to break even. These 110 units would represent the new Minimally Acceptable Production (MAP), resulting directly from the government program. This is theoretically possible if the government worker facilitates markets in such a way that allows the workers left behind to be more productive, but the initial production deficit still must be overcome in order for the government program to be justifiable. If the public program is truly worth its salt, the market will actually be able to produce more with the resources left behind. This desirable situation would represent a Preferred Efficiency Contribution (PEC). This improved rationale for evaluating government programs raises the bar for new public projects when productive resources are being removed from the private sector.

For every government worker (currently there are approximately 19.5 million and growing) that we pull out of the production process, our economy is smaller than what it could have been, and everything costs more than it would have if the resource(s) had not been removed. For every acre of land, amount of labor, dollar of capital, or entrepreneurial initiative that private industry was using, or would have used, the siphoning off by government creates a production deficit. The work of the government employee can only indirectly add value to the market, and only if his/her activity facilitates the market in such a way that the resources left behind can overcome the production deficit created and produce more goods and services prior to the initial removal.

Now, if you only have one government employee for every hundred or so workers, it is probably manageable and possibly even beneficial. But our government has grown in quantum leaps. Now, approximately one-third of our GDP runs through some government entity (BEA, 2008). A ten percentage-point increase in government expenditures as a share of GDP is associated with approximately a one percentage-point decline in the growth rate of real GDP. [4] This tidbit of information comes directly from a U.S. joint economic study.

Instead of trying ways to reduce the role of government and thereby minimize inefficiency, the president

[4] http://www.house.gov/jec/growth/function/function.htm

and U.S. Congress are looking for ways to expand their reach. This seems to be the wrong direction when forty percent of the land resource is government owned, making it unavailable for private production; financial capital is being sucked down like a YooHoo to finance record deficits; and government agencies are actively seeking out our most talented workers, paying almost $20,000 more than the private industry averages. This last one is often overlooked when we talk about the government trying to hire the best and the brightest. I want to say for what it costs to hire these "best and brightest" and the lost innovation for the private sector, maybe it would be better for government to look for the "dumb and the dimmest." At least the production deficit that would have to be overcome would a lot less at the outset.

With Principle 1 in mind, the decision making bias for or against a government program should be one of minimalization, taking into account the inefficiencies inherent with any government's use of private resources. Since government is inherently inefficient, it stands to reason that we should strive for as little inefficiency as possible. But inefficiency is not likely going to be our biggest concern. Thomas Jefferson understood that another, even more ominous inherent characteristic of government was the threat to freedom. He said, "A government big enough to give you everything you need is big enough to take everything you have." What should the government do? We are almost ready to address that very issue, but not just yet. We first must address the issue of why government spending is not the same as you spending your own money.

2

Government spending your money is not the same as you spending your own.

In undergraduate economics, I was taught that if government took your money and then spent it, the resulting expenditure balanced circular flow. Bottom line: government spending was the same as you spending your own. As a college student I obligingly accepted this as true. But, later on in life, having worked for corporations and operated my own business, I began to realize that government spending my money was much different than me spending it. Certainly not near as enjoyable, but economically speaking, government spending creates distortions and inefficiencies that are worth our consideration.

Government takes a portion of the money that you earned, and then spends it on your behalf. I usually get one of three reactions to this statement: 1) "Really?" (Shock from someone who is new to the world of work and reality, usually between the ages of six and twenty-one). 2) "Tell me about it!" (Anger from someone who is frustrated at being sucked dry by the government.) Or 3) "As is necessary." (Someone who has been taken care of all his/her life or buys into the notion that government is responsible for the individual.)

It should be said that some of those government expenditures can prove very effective at improving economic growth and raising the overall standards of living. Generally found to be more beneficial in emerging countries than developed ones, several quantitative studies have shown governments that introduce legal systems, facilitate markets, create usable infrastructure, or provide law enforcement are desirable. However, as the Rahn Curve suggests, more is not necessarily better. This economic model provided that once government passes an "optimum percentage" of the gross domestic product, increased government size retards economic growth. Experts may disagree as to whether the optimum percentage is 15 to 20 percent, but I don't think any of them would be amenable with a United States government whose debt may surpass 100 percent of the gross domestic product in 2010 and whose budget continues to barrel out of control.

Why is government spending your money different than you spending your money? The first reason is that government spends money on goods and services that you are unlikely to purchase yourself. This redirected spending could be office equipment or foreign aid or playground equipment. Your money could also be spent on the welfare program or for unemployment benefits. When Congress passes a law that takes money from you, and then they spend it, they have collectively decided they know better where that money should be spent. When the federal budget is in the trillion of dollars, this act alone reeks of hubris. I would think that a normal reaction to handling someone else's money would be one of frugality and caution. But that does not seem to be the case. From an economic standpoint, this activity alters the supply and demand, creating a false market.

Businesses that would have been rewarded with your dollar votes are shut out, and government encourages the supply of whatever it chooses. This is a big encouragement when we are referring to the huge amounts of money spent by local, state, and federal governments. In many cases, entire industries are built around the government's decision to buy products and services. Is it any wonder that individuals, companies, foreign governments, illegal immigrants, criminals, local governments, and every other conceivable type of organization are lining up at the trough to get some of this? Plato was credited with saying that democracy cannot survive once the people figure out that they can vote themselves money from others.

The federal government is currently scheduled to spend over a trillion dollars. This activity creates distortions in the markets. These distortions could logically result from the absence of the normal risk and reward relationship of the market transactions. Also, government expenditures don't involve the emotional equity of someone who had to work for the money being spent. One could imagine that this is one reason that the infamous boondoggles are chosen. To the point, would you have spent your money the same way that Department of Homeland Security funds were recently spent? As reported by U.S. Representative Anthony D. Weiner, they spent funds on: security cameras in a fishing village in Alaska; a tactical robot for Peoria, Illinois; kennels for stray animals in Modoc County, California; a grant in Kentucky to protect bingo halls from terrorists; bulletproof vests for dogs in Ohio; on-site paging system for the state agricultural fair in South Dakota; a custom trailer for the October Mushroom Festival in Texas; or fire department clowns and puppet shows in Wisconsin. For me, the clowns and puppet shows may have been worth it because any potential terrorists were likely very confused by the clever feint.

Economic theorists have provided that government officials have similar motives to those in business when it comes to expanding their domain. But it should be obvious to most the normal cost in the cost-benefit scenario is left out when it comes to government spending because the cost does not come from their pockets. That does not necessarily mean the citizens benefit. Why else would we get funding for the $1.95 million Charlie Rangel Center for Public Service? Why would the 2008 federal budget include over 11,600 special little projects that boggle the senses and cause bile to form in the back of most people's throats? It is so nice that we can spend $1.7 million dollars on sorghum research and $200,000 on the study of greenhouse lettuce germplasm. Since 1985, the government has spent over 67 million dollars trying to develop a sustainable domestic shrimp industry in the United States. Whether it is 1.1 million for Mormon crickets in Nevada or 3.4 million to protect the harbor seal and stellar sea lion, it makes normal people shake their heads in disgust and wonder why.[5]

Politicians make decisions (as do we) based on the cost of something versus the benefit. The big problem here is it is not costing government officials anything. And it appears that it has become a game of who can spend the most, which determines the politician's relative success. To make matters worse, they are not only spending what money you send in; they are splurging on borrowed money and sticking you with the interest.

You make decisions based on cost benefit. Business makes decisions based on cost benefit. This combination

5 http://www.cagw.org/site/PageServer?pagename=reports_pigbook2008

works very well in the market when there is true cost and risk associated with the decision. Buyers pursue their best self-interest, as do businesses. The market price and competition act as a regulator in the exchange. Both parties come out well. The use of the term *politicians* paints with a broad brush that is not completely fair. If you want to, you can look up your federal representative on the Citizens Against Public Waste Web site to see if you have a Taxpayer Superhero or a Super Porker. I will tell you that there are more Super Porkers and the Superheros are few and far between. Why is that?

Imagine that you have been given a near-limitless credit card and move a long way from home. To keep your card, you just have to buy some goodies for your well-placed friend back at home. Most everything you buy can remain private because no one is really paying attention to the bill. Your friends will be thrilled and help you get elected over and over again. In fact, much of what you purchase is bought with money that someone has lent the government or someone else has paid in tax. Somewhere off in magic land, there lies an accounting of all the expenditures that the federal government has made. I once wrote the shameless thief will eventually blame his victim for his actions. But this may be more like a drunk, awakening from a binge hangover; his excuse will be that you should have never trusted him with the credit card.

Assuming a benevolent government, even the most conscientious bureaucrat would not likely be emotionally attached to the money being spent the same way as the person who worked for it. The result of this distortion seems to be that the further the earning moves from the spending, the crazier the end result may become.

Secondly, this principle refers to the fact that someone has to do the taking and spending for government, meaning that there are bureaucrats who get paid to take and bureaucrats who get paid to spend. If this was a charitable transaction and we would voluntarily give the money directly to the person who ultimately would get it anyway, the economy would, at least, get all of the dollar value introduced into the economy. However, this is not what happens. The government bureaucrat is really just a middle man that passes along a portion of the tax. The payroll that is required for government bureaucracy is another difference between your spending your money and government spending it.

This concept applies to every bureaucrat and elected official, but it is obvious that in most cases it could be argued that the money would not be directed toward the need or activity that society has deemed absolutely necessary. This in a way makes the earlier point of the principle that addresses market distortion more tangible. We as citizens probably would not spend money to support the multitude of agencies and organizations that have risen like swamp water during a flood.

The sheer volume of government employees has becomes a real concern with 179 federal agencies and 1.8 million federal employees, which makes the federal government is the nation's largest employer, according the Bureau of Labor Statistics (BLS, 2009). This includes the Internal Revenue Service (IRS), which has over eighty-five thousand employees; the Environmental Protection Agency's seventeen thousand; and the U.S. Education Department's forty-two hundred. But all of those fall short of the Veteran Affairs (239,000), Homeland Security (149,000), U.S. Treasury (109,000; includes IRS), Justice (105,000), and Agriculture (92,000). The Department of the Interior (66,000; includes EPA), Health and Human Services (60,000), Transportation (53,000), and the Commerce Department (39,000) (BEA, 2009) add a few more to this all-encompassing leviathan.[6]

All of these government employees are working and getting paid. Their salaries represent an extra layer that exists when choosing public programs. In the free market each of the layers of the production process introduces value that exceeds the cost. When government removes its share, this action represents a decrease in the value of the original contribution. It does not mean the government option is never chosen; it just needs to be understood that the taking of money from one to give it to another represents a bureaucratic value loss. This should lead us to ask the question, is there a more effective way of providing a benefit or respond to a need?

Charity Navigator estimates that nine out ten charities spend less than 33 percent of the intake on administration.[7] With the Health and Human Services branch of the government spending $800 billion dollars (up 40 percent since 2006), it would be nice to know what actually makes it way back into the hands of the needy. Our decision to choose the public option should also weigh a Federal Reserve report that found a negative correlation between government spending and charitable giving.[8] It is likely that people are less charitable when their government is taking so much in taxes. Government would seem

---

6 Visit http://www.opm.gov/

7 http://www.charitynavigator.org/index.cfm/bay/content.view/cpid/48.htm

8 http://research.stlouisfed.org/wp/2007/2007-012.pdf

to not only to be a poor choice compared to charities but also serves to dampen the desire to give freely.

Government spending is not the same as you spending because it eliminates your preferences and discernment. Further, the cost-benefit and risk-reward equation is thrown off kilter. Finally, when government takes money from you and spends, there is a built-in value loss because bureaucrats require a salary to do the taking and spending. But reduced liberty, distorted markets, and value loss are not the only economic consequences of the use of government. The next principle addresses the issue of the loss of purchasing power, which goes hand in hand with more government.

3

When government passes laws, prints too much money, or goes into debt, it causes inflation.

Any time someone makes the statement, "Prices are always going to go up!" I want to ask "Really? Why do you say that?" Prices actually tend to be forced down by competition and technological advances. So why do we see prices go up and our purchasing power drop? This principle gives three causes of inflation, and our government has its hand in all three. Using the word hand is comparable to saying Bill Clinton had an eye for the ladies or that Donald Trump's hair looks a bit odd.

Just passing a law increases prices? How can that be? Our city council decided that we had a cat problem in our city. They passed a leash law for cats. Besides being unfamiliar with the nature of cats, the city council thought that the fines could be used in the city budget to pay for some programs that would help reduce the cat population. So how does that raise prices?

Every cat owner now has to buy a leash, presumably (not to mention the trips to the doctor to close up cuts and lacerations). The city will have to hire a staff to monitor the activities of the cat world. Vehicles will need to be purchased, and I think that the cat patrol should have uniforms. Also, the cat patrol will need training on how to question these cats. Yes, interrogation techniques will be necessary to find out who the owners are and why the cat is not restrained. The cat patrol may need to be armed because some of these cats or the owners may become violent when confronted. The cat patrol will need an office to work out of; and, of course, you will have to have a cat patrol management team. We will need to have an advertisement campaign that educates the owners and the cats. A computer system will have to be developed to keep track of these offenders because we may need to have some type of rehabilitation program. The court system will have to be increased to handle the caseload, and a kitty jail for those cats that are rounded up. The people jails will have to house the repetitive offenders and the violent criminals who lash out at the cat patrol. If a cat patrol officer is attacked either by cat or human, this will fall under the category of an assault of a public official, possibly a violation of federal laws. Universities can initiate studies on recidivism and apply for federal grants. There may be a need for some new federal guidelines on the safety of cat collars and the appropriate length of the leash. If the collar is not properly constructed, the cat may suffer undue psychological stress. Further, if the leash is too long, we may be in danger of accidentally choking ourselves. This should be remedied with a warning label.

Whether it is garage sale permits, parking laws, inspection stickers for automobiles, or funding for the arts, or cat patrols, your price tag just went up.

When government prints new money, the overall value of goods produced doesn't necessarily keep pace. Take the inflation created by not having as many workers producing, and add this amount to the total inflationary cost of government. Granted, the United States has a good handle on the printing of its currency (third-world countries, not so much). I do note that if the value of the dollar begins to drop globally and some of the 60 percent of the total U.S. currency (which is held abroad) ever starts flooding back into the United States, our pricing may go nuts. For clarification purposes, pretend that a nation called Pretendia produces one billion dollars in goods and services and, for simplicity's sake, has one billion in currency. The government needs money for a new welfare program and prints another billion. The money is mailed out in envelopes to all of the poor people of Pretendia. The businesses are swarmed with shoppers, and everyone hails their president as a genius. In a few months, the demand for products causes the markets to react, and prices go higher. In fact, when goods and services are not expanded to match the doubling of the money supply, the existing goods and services will logically cost twice as much. The benefit has become negligible.

The loss of purchasing power of the dollar was made clear to me by one of my former coworkers, a remarkable little science man. He stood five feet tall and possessed a completely receding hairline. His hair often stuck out from the sides as if charged by electricity, and he walked with severe gimp. One day, he was walking down the hall with a fisted hand outstretched toward me. "You know what I have here?" he asked. Knowing his proclivity for gross little bugs and creatures, I just gave an uncomfortable smile and took a step back. Oblivious to my visible reaction, he continued. "Dr. Dan, I have in my hand a silver quarter." I sighed and raised my eyebrows in a patronizing way. He asked, "You know what this would have bought me when I was growing up?" I responded with a visual no. "A gallon of gas." I gave a look of amused understanding. "You know that I could sell this quarter and get enough money to buy a gallon of gas today. His point was the silver is worth the same. It's the money supply that has lost its value." I thought, *Not bad for science guy.* The little man flipped the coin in the air and gave a big smile, knowing that he hit a topic that was of interest to me. He made a quick hundred and eighty-degree pivot on his bad leg and said, "Have a good day, Dr. Dan."

Money loses value when its relative scarcity is reduced or its growth outpaces production. Printing money too fast then just causes prices to go higher. The United States does a fairly good job of controlling the actual physical money supply, but printing money and passing legislation is not the only culprit for price going up. In the case of the United States, the creation of Federal Reserve-generated smoke and mirror money has been substituted for the printing presses. Imagine what will happen to prices when a trillion dollars of play money created by the Federal Reserve (to help us out of this economic recession) is introduced into a thirteen trillion-dollar economy.

Inflation becomes even worse when government goes into debt. Take the inflation discussed before and add to this the government debt-generated inflation. Government creates an artificial demand when it spends borrowed money for goods and services. More demand and no corresponding increase in production causes inflation. The government competes for goods and services in the marketplace, driving up prices. Could this be a major reason that prices have doubled since 1990 and quadrupled since 1972? Yep. According to InflationData.com, what cost 9.9 cents in 1913 costs about $2.02 in today's market.[9] Go see your eight-dollar movie and eat your five-

9 http://inflationdata.com/Inflation/Consumer_Price_Index/Historical-

dollar hamburger (which will cost more on the left and right coasts due to lots of regulation).

But what is wrong with a little inflation? Politicians would rather have a little inflation if it means lower unemployment. Here's the problem. Inflation deteriorates the value of the currency (i.e. a two-dollar pack of gum), but it also creates a whole set of inefficient activities in response to the rising prices. Consumers feel the need to spend quickly, creating an escalating price scenario that tends to be self-perpetuating. Higher prices beget higher prices, if you see my point. Fixed wages, including retirement incomes, don't keep up with prices; and social programs have to be adjusted. Banks have to add inflation premiums to loans; otherwise, they will, in effect, lose money. Savers are discouraged from holding reserves because they are losing purchasing power. Lower savings deposits cause interest rates to go higher, driving up the cost of borrowing. When interest rates go up, the break-even point for new business development is increased and discourages new production. Less production and innovation fosters higher prices. There is a more insidious consequence of inflation that is often overlooked. That is a hidden tax that impacts the retired community, middle and lower class workers. The loss of purchasing power is driving people to call for more help from the very people that are causing the inflation in the first place.

When we are told that government has to battle higher prices, it is like a man who pushes you in the icy water and then offers you a towel because you are cold and wet. Government's excessive legislation, overprinting of money, and taking on debt are all contributing to higher

CPI.aspx?rsCPI_ currentPage=2

prices. Ben Franklin once offered us this piece of wisdom, "Think what you do when you run into debt; you give to another power over your liberty."

As the government continues to grow unrestrained, the next principle acknowledges the Field of Dreams, saying, "If you build it they will come," but with a twist. "If you create a government program they will come."

4

Where there is a soup line, there will be a line for soup.

When our federal government moved to extend unemployment benefits from six months to twelve months, it put a burr in my blanket—not that I have anything against the unemployed. I have been unemployed. When Emery Air Freight was bought out by Consolidated Freightways (CF), the new owners fired all mid and low level managers across the country. It seems that the upper level management had already escaped with a nice parachute. Evidently I was too low on the totem pole to be given a parachute. Our little CF hatchet party took us out to dinner the night before. I now lightly refer to it as the last supper. The next morning, they took my boss, Mike, into his office and met with him. When he came out of the office, I knew from the look on his face that he was history. I felt so bad for him. He said that they wanted to talk to me in his office. I figured that they were going to justify Mike's firing. When the little man closed the door, he said that he had been reviewing my records. I thought this was a good thing; my reviews had been exemplary. For a moment, I thought that they were going to move me into Mike's position. What a moral dilemma! Needless to say, the situation was not something that I had to deal with for long. He said, "We are going to have to let you go." It was a full hit below the belt. I was out of the office by 11:00 a.m.—no severance, no expense account, no company car, no thanks for your five years of service. The new team was waiting in a nearby hotel for the slaughter to be cleaned up. With a baby on the way and no job, it was obviously a character building moment. One which we survived, I might add, but the going was anything but easy.

So I have sympathy and empathy for those who lose their jobs. But I also know intuitively that if you extend benefits from six to twelve months, you will have a group that will go unemployed for six months longer. A safety net becomes a reason for less urgency. It was at this point that I came up with the soup adage. To emphasize that point, in 2004, when Bush 43 refused to extend federal unemployment benefits, New York Congressman Charlie Rangel called it mean-spirited and irresponsible. One reporter entitled an article "Compassionate Bush to NY Unemployed: Get a Job." It must have worked because from March of 2004 for the next four years the unemployment rate in New York started on a downward trend from a high of 6.3 percent to 4.3 percent in March of 2007 (BLS).

The idea that people will line up for benefits is nothing new but still very important to understand the economic implications of the use of government. And don't be fooled by this principle's use of the phrase soup line thinking that it just applies to the impoverished or the unemployed. The soup line is not just serving squatter's soup; it is serving up Bird's Nest soup that could be served in the finest of restaurants in the way of government contracts. In fact, there is a whole gaggle of well-heeled groups that have learned the game very well. I would encourage you to read a book called, *Free Lunch* by David Cay Johnston. Walmart has certainly learned to line up at the tax trough. George W. Bush and the Texas Rangers and many other sports franchises figured out how to soak the system. But before you go blaming business, none of this could have even been in play if it weren't for the government sweet deals.

For a government whose intent is to create a level playing field, it is not difficult to see how ineffective government is. I would argue that if income equality was one of the goals of the government (it should not be, by the way), the U.S. federal government has been instrumental in creating a U.S. distribution of income that is (as Johnston claims) more representative of a third-world nation. Lyndon Johnson's 1967 war on poverty has turned out to be the assault on the middle class. It happened because smart people can take advantage of complicated laws. The rich get richer because the poor can't afford lawyers and accountants to figure out all the profitable loopholes in rules or opportunities. Legislators should realize that whatever program is created, people will adjust their activities to take advantage of the program. That program becomes the basis for a new rationale. Some people and organizations are quite adept at saddling up to the feed bag and having a big ole chew. That goes for individuals, groups, organizations, and corporations as well, because each will continually seek out what they perceive as their own best self-interest. That means that if you create a funded program for left-handed, bald-headed bird callers, you are going to have a bunch of people shaving their heads, practicing with their left hand and whistling at the trees; and the soup line continues to grow.

5

Every law passed creates the need for an additional law and it is going to cost you money and your freedom.

Because you are sneaky, that's it, "You law-bending, rule-breaking derelict." The law is not five minutes old, and you have some smarty pants trying to figure a way around it. For those tighter laws, it takes a little longer. But like a river that has been dammed, water will work to penetrate the structure, look to go over, through, under, or around. It is the job of thousands of corporate lawyers to do just that—anticipate what laws are going to be passed and how to best take advantage of them. After all, there is money to be made when the government is able to take earnings away from the masses and then pay business. Businesses and organizations look around to find the pools of money and then conform to the government requirements and start collecting. Everyday people seek out their greatest payment as well, whether it is Welfare, Medicare or any other program.

If you need more evidence of the perpetuation of laws, go no further than the Internal Revenue Service tax code. According to a leading provider of tax information, CCH, the U.S. tax code consists of more than sixty-seven thousand pages. According to government sources, eighty-five thousand employees are required to enforce the massive collection of nonsense (USOPM, 2009). The most recent tax rebate by Bush 43 was intended to stimulate the economy. It cost \$42 million just to process the checks.[10] And then, the inevitable waste of answering these questions: Who gets it, and how will it be delivered? (You will need a law.) How are we going catch the ones who are trying to get it who aren't supposed to receive the check? (You will need some more laws.) Should illegal immigrants get a check? (Another law.) How about someone who has never paid a dime? How about the criminals? Shouldn't they get a rebate check too? Guess we will have to have a law that covers all of that.

We benefit from bureaucracies. Stop lights and traffic regulations are forms of bureaucracies. Bureaucracies are necessary when dealing with large groups of people. Bureaucracies build systems that eliminate exceptions. Anytime an exception is exposed, the bureaucracy reacts with a law that removes the exception. Take the Americans with Disabilities Act. Some may think that I don't feel the access of handicap persons is important. Nothing is further from the truth. I think that businesses that make their stores more accessible will garner new customers and be known as customer friendly. I like customer friendly and will reward them with more of my business. Other businesses will see the benefit and may choose to competitively respond. If you want to pass a law, you can do that, but just realize that won't be the end of it. With each law, like a eating a Lay's potato chip, you can't just stop at just one. And we must realize that there are significant costs associated with this type of legislation and the parade of laws required to patch the holes it creates.

---

10 http://www.usatoday.com/news/washington/2008–03–07-rebate-letters_N.htm

For example, I parked in a Walmart parking lot and was almost up to the store. In whips a little sports car with a knockout blonde behind the wheel. I see her place a handicap placard on her car dash, and then she practically runs by me into the store. She was definitely not handicapped in any form or fashion. She probably could have gotten any spot in the parking lot if she asked any of the guys in the store. But she somehow had finagled one of the permits. The government now has to have review procedures to determine who is actually handicapped. Each permit requires a doctor's note, a form, and a fee.

Not too long ago, the police department put together a task force that would drive around and write tickets. A fine system had to be worked out. But since one person's handicap is another's minor annoyance, it is difficult to determine who should be really getting the handicap permits. I am sure that this is not true, but I have heard of companies that will provide a good likeness of a handicapped placard that can be purchased for a small fee.

Compliance costs are also a result of more laws. Businesses were required to allocate parking spots, provide signage, and expand or reconfigure toilet facilities and entrances. There had to be some way to enforce the rules, so the building codes had to be rewritten. And it goes on and on and on. Regardless, the taxpayers and customers inevitably foot the bill when these types of gyrations perpetuate themselves. How about just starting over with Fulghum's "All I really need to know, I learned in kindergarten" and throw the rest out?

6

When government begins trying to protect us from ourselves, we are all in trouble, and you will be paying for it.

It occurs to me that people are smarter than politicians give them credit for being. Our current government has decided that we, as citizens, are not very smart. In fact, we are so stupid that we have to be forced to put on safety belts; be told what we can and cannot eat and drink; and warned about what to buy and not buy. Government has passed age restrictions, movie ratings, warnings, and laws that subtly say, "You are just too stupid to know what is best for you, and we are going to look after you." This does not come without a price. In fact, every time one of these well-intentioned legislators dreams up another way to help you out, your wallet will feel a little thinner. My first response to this is, "Please don't do anything else for me. I can't afford any more help."

Secondly, I think I can look around and figure out what I want to spend my money on. If people are dying from it, I will try to avoid it. Believe it or not, I figured out that if I have an auto accident at seventy miles an hour, my momentum will carry me through the window. I started to religiously wear a safety belt when my brother had a fairly severe accident. He went up into the rearview mirror, requiring many stitches and some cosmetic surgery. That did it for me. I don't need a policeman pulling me over to give me a ticket for not wearing a seat belt. I felt it was my job to teach my son to wear a safety belt by example. If he does not, he may have to learn his own lesson. The notion that government is supposed to protect us from ourselves drives up the cost to produce, buy, own, and operate a vehicle.

There is also an issue beyond economics, the elimination of self-reliance and reduction of freedoms. Government protecting us from ourselves causes us to become reliant on others to tell us what is best. We have moved from the mentality of buyer beware to government approved. If I tell my children they are not old enough to see a PG-13 movie because of the rating, I am basically abdicating my authority as a parent to some higher authority rating system. Once you start down the road of protecting people from themselves, it costs money because there is always one more safety harness, or one more warning, or more rules that will make life safe. You will have to pay people to make decisions for making the decisions you once made. And once you have begun to turn over responsibility, it is hard to stop because life is inherently risky and you can't possibly anticipate every idiotic thing someone will do. When you try, you will end up with warnings on lawn edgers that read, "Do not trim your trees with this machine." Hot coffee: "Caution. This drink is hot." "Remove child before folding the stroller." "Do not put any person in this washing machine." "Do not iron while wearing shirt." Letter opener: "Safety goggles recommended." Fishhook: "Harmful if swallowed." Are you kidding me? Nope. That is where we have arrived—government trying to protect us from everything. Businesses react when the courts follow suit by punishing a company for something stupid that a consumer does with a product.

My friends, we have moved away from self-reliance to

a nanny state, costing you money and your freedom along the way. When it comes to protecting me from me, I think I would like the government to leave *me* alone. If I make a mistake, I will learn from it. If I buy a product from an unscrupulous merchant, I will not let it happen again, and I will go tell anyone who will listen not to buy from that company. I want to tell government, "Please don't do me any more favors. I can't afford your help." If you think you want the government to try to protect you from others, I understand. Certainly, national defense and police fit well into the responsibility of government.

As soon as I abdicate my responsibility for looking out for myself, I become subject to the worst affliction that can affect a populace: reliance and a sense of entitlement. It is a sure way to slide on into an all-encompassing cradle-to-grave government with little chance that your free market will survive. Your once proud and free nation may become docile and compliant. If we continue on this path, the U.S. may become a great takeover candidate for someone with power and riches on their mind.

When you hear some well-meaning person say, "There ought to be a law," hold on to your wallet, because you will be sharing the cost of enforcement and compliance. What they are really saying is that they don't like that someone is acting in a certain way, and since they can't stop them, government should. I feel your pain when someone seems to be getting away with something and not suffering the consequences, but be careful what you ask for. You will find that once you have invited government into your home or business, it is like having your mother-in-law move in with you. She will want a say on everything, and it won't be cheap.[11]

---

11 Disclaimer: I have a very nice mother-in-law.

7

Using fiscal policy to correct the economy is like trying to change the weather.

Ever notice how the economists and meteorologists have similar jobs? On the nightly news the economic fore-caster predicts the stock market is looking good or that unemployment is trending down, only to have the Dow Jones average drop the next day and unemployment numbers go up. You tune in to the evening news to watch the weather report. The weatherman, using his skill and best judgment, predicts sunny skies. What he does not know is that an unforeseen change in atmospheric pressure has caused a band of rain clouds to spontaneously form. You get to work just as the temperature begins to drop and the raindrops come down. Raising your fist to the sky, you let out a cry of confusion and express your anger at the stupid weatherman. First of all, get a real problem. Then realize that the entire weatherman's training and experience, similar to the economist's expertise, was not enough to accurately predict the ever-changing environment. If you find that the weatherman is wrong more than he is correct, you may want to consult the *Farmer's Almanac*. It seems to be amazingly accurate by simply looking at past weather patterns, without all the high-tech stuff. If your financial prognosticator is seldom correct, maybe you should give it a shot yourself. Go get a history book because you may have a better sense of what is actually happening in the economy than the experts.

The salient point in all of this is that the difficulty in anticipating what the economy is going to do relates to our expectation of what government can and cannot do for the economy. Unpredictable markets (which are made up of consumers and businesses that react to the changes in ways that are difficult to anticipate) make fiscal policy very difficult at best. And yet we are still looking to government to fix the social and economic issues. There are so many variables and factors that make it very difficult, with any certainty, to accurately predict what will happen and even more unlikely that government can have a positive impact. We have tons of experts that do nothing but research and study economics. I am not denigrating economists in any way. I consider myself an economist without a pedigree, but when students ask me what is going to happen, I always tell them that the past is the best predictor of the future, but there are no guarantees. I have come to realize that utilizing fiscal policy to correct a problem or help a specific group, particularly at the federal level, is probably the least desirable choice.

Neo-classical economists and specifically Monetarists have recognized the ineffectiveness of fiscal policy trying to impact the economy. As hard as we might try, it is nearly impossible to figure out what should be done, takes an inordinate amount of time to get legislation passed, and then more time to implement the policy or program. I would also point out the side effects are often worse than the initial ill. Efforts by the federal government to control or to successfully manipulate the economy appear to actually be counterproductive in most cases. Perhaps we need a warning label on all fiscal policy efforts such as: This stimulus check will likely cause prices to go higher, reduce your overall standard of living, and create a debt burden for future generations. After reading this warning, you may feel irritable or dejected. If your dejection lasts for more than four hours, seek immediate medical attention. Monetarists provide that governments would be better off just agreeing on a preferred growth rate for gross domestic product—setting the growth of the money supply to that rate and then get the heck out of the way. I do not contend that the fiscal policy of U.S. government is completely unable to affect the economy. Just that the economy is enormously complex, and a short run bump is probably the best that the government can hope for when implementing fiscal policy. I do believe that most of what government is able to do is ineffective in the long run, hurts as many people as it helps, and creates as many or more problems than it might solve.

How can government's effort actually make things worse? According to *Investors Business Daily* and several others, the mortgage crisis can be traced back to—who else?—the federal government and the bubbles created by the expansive monetary policy and artificially low interest rates of the Federal Reserve. It seems in vogue to blame greedy mortgage companies and banks for the waves of failed home loans. But Fannie Mae and Freddie Mac were government-sponsored enterprises created by the federal government to increase home ownership in the United States. Despite warnings from several government officials, Congressmen like Senators Chris Dodd and Barney Frank shamed the rest of Congress into opening up the housing market to individuals that were unlikely to be able to pay the loan back. From the Web site "Citizens against Government Waste," the following excerpt is included.[12]

> Perhaps most damning is Chairman Frank's irresponsible defense of the activities of Fannie Mae and Freddie Mac over the years, even when it became clear that executives at the two giant government-sponsored enterprises (GSEs) had manipulated earnings statements and gifted themselves with huge bonuses based on the bogus numbers, misled regulators, and steered the companies into such shoddy condition that they posed a systemic risk to the entire financial system. Chairman Frank must regret his September 11, 2003 statement to The New York Times that Fannie and Freddie "are not facing any kind of financial crisis…[t]he more people exaggerate these problems, the more pressure there is on these companies, the less we will see in terms of affordable housing." During a 2003 committee hearing related to establishing oversight over the GSEs, he casually announced that he didn't want "the same kind of focus on safety and soundness that we have in Office of the Comptroller of the Currency and the Office of Thrift Supervision. I want to roll the dice a little bit more in this situation towards subsidized housing." We know how that worked out: the GSEs are now almost entirely owned by the taxpayers; Freddie Mac tapped the Treasury for $13.8 billion in 2008; and Fannie Mae is on deck to get $15.2 billion this year.

Anyone who disagreed with the good senators seems to have been painted as racist or un-American. Both senators pushed for more lenient restrictions and then, when

---

12 Citizens against Government Waste Web site http://www.cagw.org/
site/PageServer?pagename=news_porkerofthemonth

everything blew up, squealed foul about the greedy banks and poor lending practices. Oh my word. No wonder these two men led the push for bailouts. Using a strategy that had worked before, Senator Frank deflected blame by calling into question others' motives that criticized his mismanagement.

Bottom line is that you can seed the clouds during a drought, but you had better expect some lightning strikes and unpredictable rain resulting from your efforts. Someone might ask, "You got rain, didn't you?" I would answer, "Yes, but the forest fires burned my house and the flood washed out my farm." One should also consider that the expansionary monetary policy of the Federal Reserve has been the root cause of the dollar consistently losing value and has created the inflationary bubbles that have rocked the U.S. economy. Whether it is the war on poverty, Medicare, welfare, industry bailouts, or stimulus packages, over and over again we see the unpredictability of the markets counteract fiscal policy efforts and punish artificial increases in the money supply, creating bigger economic disasters down the road. As usual, the ones that really are being hurt by the government's push for homeownership are the poor and middle class. I am still waiting patiently for my bailout. Think it will come soon?

8

Good intentions do not necessarily lead to good legislation.

This principle recognizes that politicians and bureaucrats have good intentions. I don't think that anyone says, "Let's see how we can really screw this up." It starts with a well-intentioned person wanting to help someone out. Helping people can be a tricky proposition. Even on an individual basis, with a decision maker of above average intelligence, the wisdom to discern whether an unfortunate situation is one to let the person work out themselves versus one in which the person truly would benefit from help is tough to acquire. Government is faced with the prospect of dealing with multitudes of people and only can deal with each situation with rules.

A person can look at the whole situation and decide whether or not help is appropriate. For example, a person has a broken leg. Do they need help? Probably. Do they deserve your help? Likely. What if they broke their leg while jumping out of a moving truck? Probably deserves help, but only after a slap on the back of the head. What if he broke his leg jumping out of a moving truck while trying to escape a pursuing gang? Probably deserves help. What if the gang was a group of neighborhood patrol members who witnessed this invalid stealing from a little old lady? Probably not. A bureaucracy cannot account for all of that and has to deal with large numbers of people and situations. The government can only pass more laws to try to shore the abuse. These news laws quickly become minor obstacles to those that can alter their behavior to exploit the new rules. When making similar decisions you may not have perfect knowledge either, but you are much more likely to be careful about giving someone your hard-earned money.

My mother and father saw a man on the side of the road panhandling. His worn clothing, uncut beard, and pitiful sign were enough to twist anyone's heartstrings. My parents were on their way to lunch and decided to give the man a dollar. Later, having finished their meal at a nearby Luby's, my parents noticed the "homeless" man walking through the restaurant to take a seat at a rear booth. He was joined shortly by another man of similar dress and fastidiousness. The two men begin to pull out a cache of dollar bills from a backpack. The two divided up their collection into four piles. Two other men arrived at the restaurant to add their take for the day. The leader took his cut and dispensed equal shares for the rest of his team. My parents were appalled and told everyone they knew about the scam. Who knows what happened to the homeless squad. They may have suffered a backlash of public sentiment or not. If they did suffer losses in revenue, perhaps they moved to some other intersection or more gullible city.

My parents reacted with their judgment, but bureaucracies can only pass rules that try to apply to every situation. One nearby city suggested issuing panhandling permits. One might guess that this did nothing to prevent the problem, rather gave some individuals some entrepreneurial incentives to organize the homeless and sell the permits based on the most lucrative street corners. The bureaucratic process does not have the luxury of discernment or judgment. That is why so many strange things happen when bureaucracies try to handle problems with rules. The result is you have little school children being expelled because they brought a plastic butter knife to school, or a student is sent to a juvenile facility because he carried a cold tablet on campus without a prescription, or a school boy that was charged with a felony for forgetting to take an unloaded hunting rifle out of his trunk. Bureaucracies tend to be devoid of common sense and can only apply rules, rules that are intended to cover every possible situation so that bureaucrats do not have to make decisions, just follow the rules.

Welfare, unemployment insurance, Medicare, Medicaid, and Social Security are all well-intentioned programs. But look at what they have become. As reported in testimony before the Senate Judiciary Committee in 1995, welfare seemingly rewards unmarried women for having more babies, increases crime, and creates a culture that could work but can live acceptably or just as well on the government dole. According to Michael Tanner of the Cato Institute, eleven major studies of the relationship between the availability of welfare benefits and out of wedlock births established a statistical correlation with increased crime (p2). One could surmise that for some, receiving a welfare check removes the need to work and the free time can be used for illegal activities. Further complicating the program, the rate of "unmarried" rocketed up through the three decades following the implementation of welfare programs. It was not until the middle nineties when welfare reform (give Clinton credit for signing it) signaled the party was over did unmarried births decline.

What did we get for our welfare? Here are the results of studies related to welfare recipients, as reported in a 2001 article by Robert Rector:

> Prolonged welfare dependence reduces children's IQ levels. Dependence also reduces a child's earnings in future years; the longer a child remains on AFDC in childhood, the lower will be his earnings as an adult. Being raised on welfare also increases the probability that a child will drop out of school and will be on welfare as an adult. Analysis shows that these effects are caused by welfare per se, not simply poverty; a poor child without welfare will do better than a similar poor child with welfare.
>
> Out-of-wedlock childbearing and single parenthood are the principal causes of child poverty and welfare dependence in the United States. Children raised in single-parent families are more likely to: experience behavioral and emotional problems, suffer from physical abuse, engage in early sexual activity, and do poorly in school. Boys raised in single-parent households are more likely to engage in crime; girls are more likely themselves to give birth outside of marriage. These effects are the result of the collapse of marriage per se rather than poverty; a poor child living with a mother and father united in marriage will do better than a similar poor child living in a single-parent home. [13]

These reports lend credence to the notion that government is not the best way to improve economic conditions among the poor and in fact fosters more poverty and other social ills.

There is significant research that reports that unemployment insurance is a strong disincentive to work and,

13 http://www.heritage.org/Research/Welfare/Test031501b.cfm

if too generous, may become self-perpetuating.[14] Said differently, unemployment insurance may be abused by those who will only go looking for work when the benefits are about to run out. According to several sources, countries that have minimal unemployment insurance programs have lower unemployment rates. Conversely, societies that provide generous payments tend to have higher unemployment numbers.

Medicare and Medicaid costs have skyrocketed to a point that the programs threaten to become the highest government social program cost. It is those very costs that are driving the current push to nationalize health care. Medicare now covers such things as gym memberships and motorized wheelchairs. One commercial for motorized wheelchairs shows a lady, arms raised, celebrating her mobility, spinning in her kitchen. She says, "I didn't pay a thing for my new wheelchair!" I am happy that she is mobile, but what the commercial leaves out is that the taxpayer did pay for the chair. It sounds uncaring, but she or her family should have paid for the wheelchair, not the taxpayer. It is these types of benefits that continue to push up costs for government programs and provides the rationalization that health care is so expensive that, yes, government needs to be in charge of the medical industry.

Social security (FICA) was supposed to have been a retirement supplement, "collected in a lock box," but instead has been raped and pillaged as source of revenue by the federal government. Eighty million baby boomers must realize that the only way that they will ever see those benefits will be for the government to roll FICA into the regular income tax and tell future generations they will

14 http://www.globalpolitician.com/21957-economics

have to start a private retirement program but still pay the hidden FICA tax. By rolling it into the income tax, the IRS will be able to charge FICA on all income instead of being limited to the first $106,000. It appears that government could not resist a pool of money sitting around. Instead of exercising fiduciary responsibility, the federal government has borrowed the excess deposits to expand Social Security benefits and pay for other programs. The reality is that the U.S. government is robbing Peter to pay Paul, and the vicious cycle continues. We have to ask ourselves an economic question. Have the natural conditions of the market made Social Security an indispensable part of retirement, or has the funding and expansion of Social Security altered the market so that people can't afford to live without the program? I am still waiting for the brave soul that takes on the Social Security Administration and those that have robbed the piggy bank.

It is hard to say where the U.S. would be without the social programs, but Adam Smith said, "The highest level of prosperity occurs when there is a free market economy and a minimum of government [involvement]." As well intentioned as these programs are, it would be preposterous to pretend that these programs have not ballooned way beyond the original intent. One could argue that they have not been absolute black holes, but most studies that I have come across show an absolute correlation between welfare programs and increased poverty, employment benefits and increased unemployment. This leads me to ask the question of whether our experience with government, being the collector of taxes and purveyor of benefits, is the best alternative. According to an England Charities Foundation study, the United States is already the world's most generous nation. Certainly some people will move in and out of need over different periods of their lives, but perhaps this represents a challenge to families and charitable organizations to increase their efforts to help those in need, not a rationale for more government.

9

Trade is good, with one exception.

Trade has increased significantly over the past decade. While world GDP's have increased at an average of 3 percent, international trade has increased at a 9-percent clip.[15] Why is that? Several reasons could be pointed out: increased ability to communicate, improved financial networks, increased transportation capacity, sustained relative world peace, improved technology, and increased number of negotiated trade agreements. However, the trade increases would not have happened if there had not been an overall acceptance of the benefit of trade. This is not to say that there are not any negatives; but in the intermediate and long run, the benefits far outweigh the negatives. One only has to look at the NAFTA agreement for verification. (By the way, give credit where credit is due; Bill Clinton signed this into law.)

According to the Office of Trade Representative (USTR), from 1996 to 2006, trade among NAFTA nations has increased from $297 billion to $883 billion, an increase of 198 percent. Exports to the NAFTA partners represent 35 percent of the total U.S. exports. This agreement has been particularly positive for agricultural numbers for both the U.S. and Mexico.[16] Mexico has come so

---

15 World Trade Organization numbers. http://www.wto.org/english/ res_e/statis_e/its_e.htm 2009 numbers have dropped, but the previous trends were up.

16 http://www.ustr.gov/assets/Trade_Agreements/Regional/NAFTA/ Fact_Sheets/asset_upload_file366_13495.pdf

far in the economic development process that one would have to be disingenuous to suggest that NAFTA has not been a success. This is not a naïve person's version of the truth. Mexico has a ways to go; but from a government and monetary system that was on the verge of collapse several times in the past twenty years, significant improvement has been witnessed. This is not only good for the citizens of Mexico but also those of the United States. You think we have an illegal immigration problem now. Let Mexico break into revolution and see how things go.

I am against illegal immigration as well as programs that are extended to illegal immigrants. These programs, whether it be education or health benefits, simply reward behavior that we supposedly are trying to discourage. I do notice that we don't have Canadians constantly trying to illegally immigrate into the United States. I asked one of my students, who happened to be from Canada, why there was not a huge illegal immigration problem from Canada to the United States. He correctly came to the conclusion that there is not a huge difference between the two economies. It is a lesson to us about Mexico. The U.S., like it or not, is attached to Mexico geographically and therefore economically. California has felt the full effect of trying to pay for illegal immigrants, immigrants, and their families, but in the last decade Texas has begun feeling a measurable impact as well. According to a Texas Education Agency report, its schools are trying to educate an increasingly impoverished population. Of the increased student population growth, 97 percent fall into the economically disadvantaged category. When the studies are examined, 94 percent of the growth in the last decade was comprised of an increase in the number of Hispanic students. One only has to look at the 58 percent increase in the English Second Language students to understand the crux of the issue.[17]

When the new health care bill is examined, one of the biggest costs will be to insure legal immigrants, their families, and illegal immigrants. According to the U.S. immigration service, the bill goes up by 60 billion dollars when these three groups are included in the coverage. If the U.S. wants to reduce illegal immigration, one improvement would be to trade more with Mexico. This will increase the overall standard of living in Mexico and create a customer for our products as well. This question comes to mind: How many computers is a third-world nation going to purchase? How many computers does an advancing country require? Securing the borders is a prudent, albeit costly, endeavor. In the meantime, I conclude that we would be wise to address the issue with Mexico, through business development activities instead of paying for a two thousand-mile wall.[18]

What is the one exception? When others do not play by the same rules, the market can not work properly. Of course, the World Trade Organization helps in some respects; but there is a real concern about simple politics corrupting the genuine efforts to trade. When politics gets involved, the market activity is stifled. Just look at the events surrounding the steel tariffs implemented by, previously "free trade" president, George W. Bush. Not only did the WTO object, the U.S. auto industry threw a hissy fit because their cost for steel shot up. A government can

17 http://ritter.tea.state.tx.us/research/pdfs/enrollment_2008–09.pdf
18 This is a controversial issue because we have a duty to protect our borders. To be clear, I am against illegal immigration. We certainly should not have government programs that encourage illegal immigration.

try to protect particular industries, but it makes for inefficiencies that are difficult to justify. The short-term pain that an industry goes through is a normal market reaction that eliminates the inefficient and rewards the lean producers. In a short-sided effort to help out the steel industry, unexpected consequences were realized that should have been predictable. Shielding one industry just puts the screws to some other industry.

Jobs will be lost when competitors produce superior products or equivalent products at a lower cost. Protectionism aside, should New York state place an embargo on Arkansas chickens because the workers in Arkansas are paid so much less than New York workers? Should the Missouri government have insisted that Southwestern Bell leave the state entirely when the company decided to move its executive headquarters to San Antonio? Should the San Antonio city council try to punish AT&T when it decided to move its headquarters to Dallas?

Unrestricted trade offers the greatest opportunity for efficient offerings of all types of products and services. I have to tell that even when jobs are outsourced, it does not mean that it will have to or does stay that way. I will never buy another Dell computer as long as their customer service remains in India. It was one of the most frustrating months of my life trying to find and replace my laptop after Dell misplaced it during a repair. I could not understand them and they could not understand me. They never did locate my computer, but to their credit, after a month of haggling, they did replace it with the very one that I am typing on now. Companies may realize that cutting costs in some areas is not worth it, begin losing profits, and may see the good old U.S. worker as a much better deal than initially thought. But notice that I did not say anything about passing a law that prevents a company from using whatever labor source they think is best. Does it work for them? The market will decide.

Trade negotiations targeted at eliminating most, if not all, tariffs and quotas should be encouraged. If you are going to try to keep heavy importing countries and heavy exporting countries on an even field, charge a small, mutually agreeable percentage on all imports, regardless of the industry. Allow comparative advantage to work in the market and the result will be businesses knowing that they have to adjust and innovate in order to compete.

This is not as easy as Captain Pickard saying, "Make it so!" This is a role of the government to negotiate on the country's behalf. Facilitation of trade, working with businesses that are exporting or desirous to do so, is an appropriate function of the government. I am not talking about this guilt-ridden apologist's approach that portrays the U.S. as the unlovable glutton. Trade relations with other countries does fall into the government's area of responsibility. Perhaps the balance that we may be served best by is a cooperative but fiduciary role of government when negotiating with other countries. In other words, it would be nice if we were confident that our team was looking after our best interest as a whole. I get nervous when I hear our current president saying that our trade agreements need to be reevaluated. It seems to me that protectionism raises its ugly head when times get tough. Look up the Smoot Hawley Tariff Act and let me know how that worked out. Me? I'll bet on the ability to compete and ingenuity of Americans. Bottom line: trade is good and should be encouraged.

10

Markets are like fresh air with an occasional but infrequent stinker.

With government? Well, you will get used to the smell. I often hear the call for government when people taking advantage of others (Enron comes to mind). This justification for regulation is usually based on the idea that the market will take advantage of us poor rubes. Actually, people are fairly savvy when it comes to their own self-interest. Go read *The Wealth of Nations* by Adam Smith, written in 1776. Even way back then, Smith understood that the best regulator in the market was self-interest. In other words, markets will usually punish the occasional stinker.

Market failure is a popular topic in today's economic world. But do markets really fail? The market deals with poor producers when they go out of business. The issue is the time that it takes the market to react. This short-run period can have some unpleasant results. For example, if you are making a drink (we'll call it "DC's Youth Boost") and it tastes bad, the market will punish you if the public does not buy it by putting DCYB out of business. If DCYB makes the consumers sick, the market will take care of your Youth Boost product as well—people will not only stop buying it, but they will actively tell others. Again, the economic short run is the time that it takes market to react. In the long run (which could be a short time away), the market works. If the drink is lethal, will the market work? The answer is yes, with the issue being the casualties in the short run. Should government regulate this drink or all drinks? Your answer may depend on your personal preferences and beliefs, but please note the markets worked ... in the long run.

Perhaps a more extreme example would help. I have always wanted to be a medical doctor. So I decide one day to give it a try. I make a sign, with my woodworking skills learned from being an Eagle Scout. Turns out I will be my first patient! And having treated my burns and cuts successfully, I am encouraged even more that I should be a doctor. I proudly place my sign outside the door of my house and begin accepting my first patients. Though traffic is slow at first, the flyers that I paid the neighbor boy to distribute yield a few clients. Let's say I do a poor job and my first patient now walks with a permanent limp. The second client's cough continues to get worse, developing into pneumonia. A third person dies from my misdiagnosis and subsequent treatment of his halitosis. The last had a sprained ankle, but his breath really needed to be dealt with and kerosene seemed like it would take care of the problem. How will the market react? Will my career as a doctor flourish? Has the market failed? The likely result is that the limping first patient will pass along his experience with Dr. Dan and at the very least warn people not to go in for an ingrown toenail. Unless, of course, if they were willing to lose a toe. My prices are less than the market's going rate. The second person will not recommend me for treatment of a mild cough, and the last guy, well ... he can't give me a referral. The bottom line is that I will go out of business eventually.

In the long run the market penalizes those businesses that don't operate ethically or effectively by not rewarding them with dollar votes, eventually forcing them out of business. The markets works! With adequate information, this is true of negative externalities and under allocated costs as well! The rub in the short run is that there may be some casualties. Buyer beware seems to be passé with our government trying to protect us from every conceivable negative consequence of consuming a product or service, and even protect us from ourselves. (To further complicate the situation, people are calling for more protection and regulation by government, even suing government for not taking enough precautions.) The real culprit here is lack of information and the usual small percentage of disreputable people. If you know that someone has been producing a harmful or poorly constructed product and you decide to buy it anyway, you made a poor decision. If everyone had good information and each person knew he/she had to look out for their own self-interest, proactive investigations would likely to return as standard practice.

It appears that we have slipped down the slippery slope of trying to protect everyone from everything—labeling, licensing, liability, legislation have moved us away from a self-reliant frame of mind. Whenever something bad happens to someone, many blame the free market and call for more government regulation. Once we as society have said, "There ought to be law," it simply means that we are giving up on the market's ability to react or that the short run casualties are determined to be too unconscionable. People that complain about the free market need to look at it in the context of whether there is any other system that works better. Remember that markets work, but sometimes it takes a while for the information to get out. In the long run, the markets do take care of products or services that people don't want to buy again. The problem is that the short-run consequences of poor consumer choices can be quite undesirable. What might be a potential role of government be in lieu of regulation? I will let you ponder that for a while.

The second issue for markets is the idea of who gets what and the issue of fairness. The market answers the question of who gets what by answering, "Who can afford it?" It seems that many people don't like that answer because it is not fair. The fairness issue is a tough one because once you begin to determine who should get what or what is minimally acceptable, the game is on. A society may decide that basic food and shelter is a minimum for everyone. So a food and housing program is started to guarantee that every person has at least food to eat and a place to live. Herein lies the problem. What is an acceptable amount, and what should the minimum standard of quality be? One does not have to look to far to find study after study that shows welfare programs are correlated to a higher poverty rates, crime, and yes, higher rates of out of wedlock pregnancies.

So what should the government be doing? I offer up the role of government in the following statement: When society decides that a product or service is absolutely necessary and the free market is unwilling or unable to produce it, that is a possible role of government. In a basketball analogy, I would characterize the role of government to be a fan and referee but not a player or owner. Can you see the similarities? As a fan, the government may facilitate markets by providing information or infrastructure.

As a referee, it establishes basic rules (legal system) and enforces the rules (judicial system). Past that point, government's role does not include being competitor; the free market will do that much more efficiently. The government does not need to become the owner of industry or resources; the market will allocate them much more effectively. The problem with a command government trying to make everything fair has been evident in almost every civilization where it has been tried. The incentive to produce and the allocation of resources is an insurmountable problem. So is the market perfect? No. But it is the best way to allow for freedom, higher standards of living, social progress, liberty, and freedom. To make the case that some people are incapable of watching out for themselves and therefore need someone wiser to take care of their needs is the most elitist and racist ideology that exists. Providing the opportunity for the pursuit of happiness and enjoying the liberty guaranteed by our Constitution is and always will be best provided by the free market.

Over the years these principles are constantly to be added to and rewritten. They are intended to cause people to think critically about the economic choices that we are making and have in front of us. The current crisis is nothing really new, but the numbers that we are dealing with are threatening the very existence of our country. We must make some tough decisions or we are looking at a financial collapse. Look back in history to see what caused the downfall of almost all societies in history and you will find it has been economics. Our country was formed in order to get out from under the English government's tyranny. During crisis, we have been conditioned to respond by calling for more government.

I think there is a substantial majority of people—yes, you—that just need a bit of a jolt to start your motor running. Sometimes I read something and I say, "I knew that. That's right, I just didn't quite put the picture together, but now I see it quite clearly." Maybe the principles have done the trick for you and you will say, "Thank you, Economic Comic, I needed that." But don't stop now. Take a look at this next section where I delve into some deeper "doo doo" economics. The danger is that you will realize that just boots won't do. With the economic shape we are in, a whole body suit is required, and we have to figure a way out of the muck and the mire.

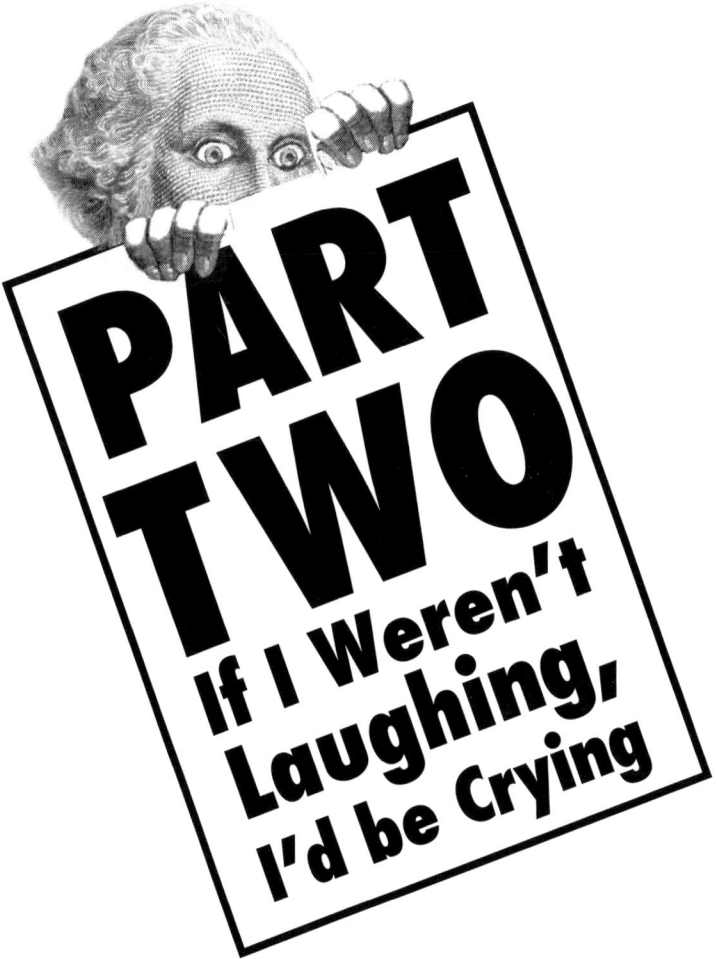

PART TWO

If I Weren't Laughing, I'd be Crying

Economic Issues and Solutions

1

The difference between charity versus a free lunch and its economic costs

More than likely your parents have told you there is no such thing as a free lunch. Someone is paying for it. Yet, for some, the lunch does in fact seem to be free for them. Further, the free lunch program is encouraged and even rewarded in some cases. Once the help becomes expected, it is no longer a gift but an obligation. To show how ridiculous this can become, one school had a contest to see which class would bring back the highest percentage of completed free lunch forms. Students were being told to fill out the form even if they didn't think they would qualify or care to participate. School officials are smart people that have figured out that all kinds of funding are tied to the number of students you have on the free lunch program. More money is allocated for teachers, as well as Title One reading fund money. Ain't it great, the federal free and subsidized lunch program was expanded in 1998 to include after-school snacks as well. It is reported that some schools provide staff and food throughout the summer months too. So for these folks, all that is left is a house on the school grounds and a ride on a school bus to the mall. Of course, the program is not free. That is the point. Taxpayers are paying for this welfare program. Today, this program serves over 30 million students in the ninety-eight thousand plus U.S. schools at a cost of $8.7 billion.[19]

My, how things have changed! When I was an elementary student, I was embarrassed that my family was asked if we wanted to be included on the free milk program, and I realize that there is still probably a negative stigma to being on the free lunch program. But wow! Have we come a long way! The good intentions have just continued to flow through our system so that everyone is provided total care. And there is someone reading this that is very upset. "You meany, mean-spirited, selfish, uncaring old man. You would deny a poor kindergartener a sandwich or a breakfast taco? You have all you need, and you want to take away probably the only food this poor little child will have today?" This is the same argument that traps most caring people that know intuitively that charity starts in the home, nonprofit organizations, and churches. Many of these people would be really upset at my mother, who recalled that those children who accepted the free lunch were required to work in the school cafeteria cleaning tables and washing dishes. I guess that she would be told that she should have kept that bit of history to herself.

Well-intentioned people ask, "If America is such a great country, shouldn't we look after the least of us? Aren't we a rich enough country that we can afford to take care of those who cannot take care of themselves? Where is your compassion and generosity?" We are the great economic powerhouse that we are because our past generations have not counted on government to help. The "aren't we rich enough" argument is the liberal mind-set that we

19 http://www.fns.usda.gov/cnd/Lunch/AboutLunch/NSLPFactSheet.pdf

must help these poor misfortunates. It is this path that has led to the current sense of entitlement that infects so many of our citizens and leads to the endless expansions of costly programs. Not only are the programs economically unsustainable; study after study shows they make the problem worse!

The United States is full of people who have been on the bottom of the economic system, and we are called to maintain the system that allows people the *opportunity* to *succeed*. We are compelled by our Constitution to maintain a limited government that guarantees people the right to *pursue* happiness. Those who need a chance or help are in a system that allows you to help yourself. Family and charity picked up where individuals could not. Government has proven to be a terrible way to organize charity. It is economically inefficient and tends to perpetuate the very situation is trying to correct.

It seems that the sense of entitlement in this country has overtaken the work ethic. This mind-set is opposite of the American spirit that this country was founded upon. I hear people actually say they have a right to an education and a right to transportation and food while receiving their education. I hear people talk about their right to have a job and right to unemployment benefits. I hear people say that they have a right to be heard. I hear people say they have a right to proper health care. Let's see. No, no, no, no, no, no, and no. The sense of entitlement leads to a society that is unmotivated and needy. And if you are against any of the government programs that supposed to help, you are characterized as selfish and uncaring and probably racist. They will get back to you on that, but definitely you are selfish and uncaring. I respond by saying,

"I don't like someone riding on my back and telling me that I am not moving fast enough." The lesson we need to revisit is: Give a man a fish sandwich and he will be satisfied for a day. Teach a man to fish and he will be able to provide for himself. Offer to fish every day for someone? You will have a line of people waiting for you to get back at the end of the day and suggesting what type and size of fish you need to catch for them.

Helping someone out is an act of compassion and charity. Accepting charity may be necessary on occasion and not a way of life. When we rely on government to provide the help, it evolves into costly obligation and inefficient use of resources. The economic control of government has been growing steadily since the early 1900s with the push for the central bank and then the public programs of the 1930s; but loss of freedoms we are witnessing today in the name of economic crises or protecting our security are pointing to our federal government being the slave owners of the twenty-first century. Using government is just a way to say: 1) that these people are not going to receive any assistance if government does not do it; 2) we as a society are unwilling to help out our family and neighbors; and 3) these people are incapable of helping themselves. If you accept those three statements, then government is the best choice, it is going to be very expensive, and I don't like the smell of it. It smells of inefficiency, entitlement, and social and moral decay.

2

Can we afford to be the policeman of the world?

If we believe that the government is our white knight in shining armor coming to our rescue, we have given into the Marxist philosophy and elitist thinking, that a few know best. From an internal perspective, this type of thinking is the same type of ethnocentricity that we have been guilty of when trying to address the issues of nations around the world. We, as the US, would be well served by the mind-set of tending our own garden. It has been the pretentious idea that we, somehow, are responsible for what happens in the rest of world, which causes us to continually get into jams. The despicable attacks of 9–11 had to be addressed, but with a deliberate strike at the perpetrators. It is amazing to me that with all of our technology and manpower Osama could not be found. I guess Rambo and Ethan Hunt were already on missions somewhere else in the world.

So what is the U.S. supposed to do when an oppressive government enslaves or kills its own people? We may be asking ourselves that very question if the U.S. government continues to grow, but our track record for covertly backing leaders does not appear to me to have been very successful. I certainly don't know all the secret alliances, but recent history has not been too kind. We have backed the Shah Reza Palavi (Iran), Daniel Noriega (Nicaragua), Saddam Hussein (Iraq), Ayub Khan (Pakistan), Yahya Khan (Pakistan), Musharraf (Pakistan), Suharto, Osama Bin Laden (Afghanistan), and Augusto Pinochet (Chile).

These are just the ones who are commonly discussed today. In Africa today, our need for oil seems to have caused us to tolerate all kinds of inhumanity. This is not an easy menu to order from. However, on the list of things to do, the federal government is in charge of our dealings with other nations. I am sure that the state department could provide a list of all our successful interventions, but it seems that we have gone from the country that others want to emulate to the country that most hate. I am not so concerned about the radical states out there and their opinions of us. If it is envy that drives their dislike, so be it. The U.S. can certainly feel good about the positives of our humanitarian efforts to help out the rest of the world. I am no apologist, but if we help someone out because of an egocentric attitude, we have moved into a whole new relationship. If it were me and the situation was reversed, I certainly do not want to accept help from someone who thinks he is better than I am. And if I have to accept the help, though I still should be grateful, I may be tempted to be bitter. I will tell you that egocentric tends to turn me off. And if someone does not want my help, hey, no skin off my nose.

We should practice the idea of being neighbors. If my neighbor comes over, I would offer him a beer. If he comes over every day and drinks all my beer, I will politely suggest that he bring his own. He is welcome to watch the television show that I am interested in; but if he wants to decide what to watch, I will ask him politely to leave. I would, on occasion, be willing to loan out a thing or two; but if I thought he was abusing my generosity, I would cut him off. If he is stealing my television set, I would reach for my shotgun. I would not open the door for him and help him out. I don't care if he is my neighbor. If he is hurting my family, same applies. If he is beating his wife or his kids, I am going to address it by stepping in or calling the police. If he is plotting to attack my house, I will take steps to protect my family and home. I will try to discourage his attack by demonstrating how far I am willing to go to protect my family and home. I would not tell the man how to run his house. If asked, I might suggest to the woman that she might be better off somewhere else; but I would not plot to get someone friendly in there to take the husband's place.

What are we to do then? I am reminded that Samuel Adams said, "What the world requires of the Christians is that they should continue to be Christians." Financially we can't afford being policeman to the world. As my dad used to say, "We can't afford it." Once he said that, I don't remember much conversation happening after that. Philosophically though, imposing our way of living on others won't be seen as welcome. As my mother said, "Don't stick your nose in someone else's business unless they ask for your help and you don't mind getting punched in the nose."

3

Inefficiencies of the U.S. personal income and corporate taxing systems

Republicans have touted tax reductions while the Democrats have fought them every step of the way. Reagan and Bush 43 were responsible for reducing taxes. Democrats complained bitterly that these cuts were irresponsible. Talk about audacity. They must have asked, how could the federal government possibly continue to spend the kind of money they were planning to spend with these boobs cutting taxes? When it was suggested that we cut government spending, the liberals called it Draconian. But honestly, income tax reductions, though welcome, don't do much good if the government simply borrows money and continues on their spending spree. Our taxing system perpetuates the problem and actually gives rise to the very economic calamities that we are facing today.

People either forget or deliberately ignore the fact that Reagan inherited an economy with high unemployment, [20] high interest rates, [21] and high inflation.[22] "Better Red than Dead" surveys were not uncommon. The top tax bracket marginal rate was at 70 percent. Within a few years, all of that mess had been turned around. Reagan

---

20 10.8% December of 1982. http://investment-blog.net/us-double-digits-unemployment-rate-of-1980–1981-vs-2008–2009-single-digit/

21 14.9% http://www.kansascityfed.org/publicat/Sympos/1985/S85BRANS.pdf

22 Inflation CPI 13% http://www.frbsf.org/education/activities/drecon/2004/0408.html

convinced a Democratic Congress to drop the top rate to 29 percent.

Many have blamed the increased deficits on the tax cuts. If those people bothered to check revenues, it would be discovered that after a year of a decreases, the tax revenue began to rise. Tax revenue returned because more people were working and investors were again encouraged to participate in the market. People forget the bad shape that the economy was in and the effect that Reagan had on this country. If the Gipper could have balanced the budget instead of signing budgets that ballooned, he would have completed one of the greatest comebacks in history. Instead, the U.S. continued down a path of fiscal mismanagement.

The problem is not the percentage of tax that one group or another pays. It is the income tax that is itself flawed. Taxing a person's productivity is not only inefficient but economically unsound. Whenever a tax is placed on something, you are going to get less of it than you ordinarily would have. Our economic system would be much better served by eliminating the income tax. If you must tax something, tax consumption. There are so many advantages and savings that one has to wonder why this idea only gets Internet coverage.

The Internal Revenue Service employs eighty-five thousand plus employees and processes over a hundred and thirty-two million household tax returns.[23] (This does not include all the contract employees and the fact that businesses are defacto forced tax collectors) Imagine

23 The IRS processes over 140 million individual, corporate, and partnership income tax returns a year as well as over 1.5 billion information returns from employers and other third parties. In total, the IRS collects over 2 trillion dollars in taxes each year.

the savings of processing only returns from businesses. [24] The IRS would only be responsible for making sure that businesses collect and submit sales tax revenues. People would no longer have to worry about filing tax returns. The paper savings alone would make the environmentalists happy. Businesses would still have to collect sales taxes, but imagine the savings of employers who would no longer have to worry about withholdings and employee tax law. Businesses are already set up to collect and submit tax collections; thus, little or no additional burdens would be added.

Wouldn't it be nice if criminals had to pay taxes on their ill-gotten gains? How many criminals do you think file income tax reports? But criminals do spend money and therefore would pay a consumption tax. Collection from criminals and drug pushers alone should be an incentive to adopt a consumption tax.

In addition, people would be more likely to save. Saving would increase bank reserves, lowering interest rates naturally, instead of having the Federal Reserve pump in imaginary money. Lower interest rates would encourage businesses' investment. Don't forget that workers get their money up front in their pocket, spending on what they

---

24 Taxpayers incur costs complying with the tax code. The IRS relies on taxpayers assessing their own income tax liability, requiring individuals to learn about the tax law, obtain appropriate forms, keep records, determine their tax liability, and submit returns to the IRS. The IRS estimates that taxpayers will spend an average of 26.4 hours preparing their 2007 tax returns and $207 on out-of-pocket expenditures (e.g., computer software, paid preparers). http://www.taxpolicycenter.org/tpccontent/healthconference_holtzblatt.pdf "The Challenges of Implementing Heath Reform Through the Tax System," Janet Holtzblatt Congressional Budget Office, February 2008

choose to spend on. Government can estimate spending based on the previous month or year of collections. I am sure that the apologetic elitists and the misguided protectors of the downtrodden will trot out the old "regressive tax" mantra. Don't be fooled. If they really knew what a regressive tax was, that same group would be attacking income limits on Social Security. They should be embarrassed to throw this red herring out there. If they were truly in it for the poor, knowing that the simplicity of a consumption tax, they should be eager to free us from the monster of the IRS. If the regressive part really concerns you, continue the tax exemption for unprepared food items (as it exists now). With changes in society's eating habits, one could argue that the food exemption should be extended to include food prepared in restaurants. But be warned, once you start down this road, everybody and their brother will be looking for ways to exempt their own products.

There are a few short-run consequences to a consumption tax but so few that objections can easily be seen as disingenuous. The tax code is over sixty-five thousand pages and requires two billion dollars' worth of the compliance time. Why would anyone insist on staying with such a ridiculous process? The only answer is that people have a financial stake in keeping things the way they are. Whether it is power or payoff, we have a whole group of people that feeds off the system like a scavenger fish following a Great White.

Similar to the U.S. income tax, the corporate income tax system is inherently flawed as well. When you study the makeup of the U.S. economy, you find that numerically business in the U.S. is dominated by small business. Better than 70 percent of all businesses are sole proprietorships. The tax laws for businesses are so complicated that only the larger corporations can afford to seek out the loopholes and benefits. Corporations represent almost eighty percent of the total sales and yet claim only 14 percent of the profits. Granted, wages and salaries are taxed, but the system rewards behavior that likely would not take place were it not for how taxes are collected.

Corporations have the revenue that allows for such expenses as large executive salaries, lavish buildings, private airplanes, prolific entertainment and expense accounts. All of these "expenses" of doing business are simply written off against income. Think how businesses would change their behavior if these expenditures were no longer tax deductible. The bottom line is that government has no business telling companies how much they should pay their employees or how they spend their money. However, through a convoluted taxing system perpetuating business decisions that are counterintuitive to good business practices, all kinds of poor business decisions start to make sense. You see, if a business makes or doesn't make a purchase should be based on whether the decision maker believes that it furthers their business effort by earning more profit. If the corporate jet increases revenue and ultimately profit, then it is a good business decision. If an executive is worth 30 million dollars, so be it. If buying NBA box seats gains you more market share, Go, Spurs, Go. The corporate taxing system, if you decide to tax business, should be based on revenues, not profits.

If government taxed revenue, how you run your company would be your business. All the government would concern itself with would be your sales. Efficiency would be rewarded and excesses would no longer be advantageous to those running businesses. Profitably operating through efficient means would be rewarded. Granted, the tax lawyers and accountants would need to alter their job descriptions or find new lines of work, but the simplicity and savings would be immediate. Many of these tax system advantages have simply unbalanced the playing field for the free market in the favor of large corporations and created real moral hazards that would not exist in a revenue tax system. My guess is that the corporate revenue tax would result in companies operating much more efficiently and create a substantially larger revenue base for the government. A revenue tax would certainly be one that encourages companies to make decisions based on the good of the bottom line rather than cause distorted behavior for the purpose of taking advantage of tax schemes.

Circumspectly, taxes are necessary for government to operate but should be collected in a way that is not time consuming or confusing. The amount of time and effort to comply with the current complicated tax codes creates confusion, distrust, anger, and avoidance. The current system also gives rise to the potential tyranny by those that are tasked with collecting the taxes. The fairest tax is a user tax, but when that is not possible, we must adopt taxing systems that reward productivity and efficiency. Abraham Lincoln said, "Prosperity is the fruit of labor. Teach economy. That is one of the first and highest virtues. It begins with saving money." Imagine this next year in the month of March you were actually thinking about how to earn or save more money, or how your company was going to make more profit instead of trying to figure a way to show as little income or profit from the previous year. Everybody, sing along, what a wonderful life it would be.

4

Should the U.S. worry about the European Union and China?

European Union

If the European Union (EU) was ultimately patterned to compete with the United States, it has gotten off to a good start. The Euro has surpassed the U.S. dollar, and the EU has become the largest trading entity in the world.[25] If the leaders of the EU are looking at the United States as their model, they may want to take a look at our history before proceeding.

The very actions that the EU executive council is trying to push through represent the same types of economic threats that the industrial North was throwing at the agricultural South. If one group perceives that the other is pulling a power play that limits economic productivity or destroys the economy, a resistance will be formed. What is to say that the EU will not have to experience the same type of growing pains that the U.S. experienced during its two hundred and thirty plus years? That means that meshing Italy and Germany might be comparable to uniting New York and Mississippi.

There's no doubt that the common currency, elimination of tariffs, and the ease of travel have been absolute positives. However, with that success, the leaders of the EU seem to believe that they have a universal mandate

---

25 http://ucatlas.ucsc.edu/trade/subtheme_trade_blocs.php

to expand their control into more and more areas. Perhaps they are looking at the U.S. federal government. Or maybe it is just the inevitable grab for power that happens when people are given authority over others. It is likely that the European Union will have to go through the same type of growing pains that the United States did when it was first formed. Certainly a civil war is inconceivable, but an economic rebellion could be an inevitable prospect. The European Union leaders should look at history and proceed with caution and patience. Take it from the Economic Comic, "When it comes to government, less is more."

China: The Millennial Version of the USSR?

In my estimation, the communist solution has not worked out so well around the world. However, you still have the Russians who are apparently oblivious to their past failure. Several of the former Soviet block think they were better off as part of the Soviet Republic. China could very well be headed down the same path.

When I was growing up, I had only one perception of what a Russian was. I did not realize that the USSR had so many distinct cultures. I assumed that all Soviets were, well, Russians. When the Soviet Union fell, all of those different groups established their identity, breaking away from the old regime (fifteen in all). Several of those new countries have moved closer to a market system. Latvia, Lithuania, and Estonia have been the most successful. The Islam-based countries have made great efforts to extricate themselves from the former Soviet Union, but their collective economic progress has been less than stellar.

It is not inconceivable that China will experience the same type of deterioration that the USSR experienced. We have already seen the cultural revolt in Tibet. With eight different languages and thirteen different ethnic groups, China is as diverse as is it large. It is this lack of homogeneity that may be our saving grace. Otherwise, the numbers, by themselves, are quite intimidating. Their 1.33 billion people include a workforce of 807 million. This includes a surplus of 35 million males.[26] Call me crazy, but this makes for a formidable fighting army. And you can bet with that many unattached males they will be feeling more than a little randy.

This fear was further confirmed when I was sitting at a friend's Christmas table. My wife and I were enjoying a delicious meal, seated next to and across from two college students on educational visas from the Republic of China. Both were extremely polite and made a considerable effort to answer the genuine questions that were being posed. I finally asked if the students planned on working in the United States once their degrees were completed. The more forthright of the two students said with no apology, "I don't think that in the long run our two countries are on compatible paths." It was an answer that made me take a quick inventory of the knives on the table.

The fact is that the robust economic information that we receive from China may be entirely overoptimistic. Without a doubt, they are selling us a tremendous amount of goods. The only advances that seem to be in place are technologies that have been borrowed or stolen from the rest of the world. There is no real proof, but the Clinton administration may have single-handedly armed the Chi-

---

26 http://cia.gov

nese defense system that will eventually be used against us. When they find out that all those treasury notes they have invested in are worthless, they may be pissed. But we can send Barney Frank, Chris Dodd, and Nancy Pelosi over there to just explain that the U.S. is just too big to fail. Hopefully by the time they figure out that we are running the mother of all Ponzi schemes, it will be too late. They will be too broke to retaliate.

5

Business-driven or consumer-driven?

The argument has been bandied about for years now whether demand or supply drives the economy. In fact, the basic notion of unfettered markets was observed way back in 1776 by Adam Smith. Jean Batiste Say, in what came to be known as Say's law, said that supply creates its own demand. In the modern day, Nobel prize-winning author, unabashed welfare state proponent, and self-proclaimed Democratic socialist Paul Krugman wrote a chapter called "Supply Side's Silly Season" (1999). He scoffed at the idea that lower taxes on the wealthy would generate growth and called it a ruse. But really this red herring is to distract us, with knowing winks and smiles that the person is crazy and of course should be dismissed from any legitimacy. The group of economists that throw out the phrase "trickle down" with a dismissive smirk are really ignoring the fact that the free market economy is driven by business and the pursuit of profit through acceptance of risk. Those that try to ignore the validity of supply side economics simply conclude that supply side economics is based only on low taxes. One would be hard-pressed to argue the turnaround that actually happened from 1980 to 1988. If one reads *Wealth and Poverty* by George Gilder (1993), you get a much more accurate picture of how the markets actually work. It is entrepreneurs taking risks that lead to consumer demand. I know that this seems like a chicken and egg discussion, but this is critical to understanding capitalism's success and the lack of viability of a command system. Marx said that capitalism could not survive because it was exploitive and power would be concentrated in fewer and fewer hands. Keynes thought that capitalism worked most of the time but needed government to step in and occasionally help things out. Both Keynes and Marx had something in common. They saw the system in terms of a game of Monopoly—a zero-sum game, as Gilder characterized the pessimist notion, where the only way one can win is at the expense of others. Both Keynes's and Marx's (and you can throw Malthus in there as well) theories saw only finite resources, a finite bank, and one winner. What both Marx and Keynes did not account for was a system that allows for the entrepreneurial spirit. They underestimated you.

My impression of the U.S. economy is that following substantial periods of unemployment, a groundswell of new businesses arises like the spring following the winter. Secondly, the meddling by government is what often perpetuates and then extends the downturn. Both Marx and Keynes both neglected to account for the entrepreneurial spirit that is fostered and created by a free-market system. Consumer demand follows business. Business responds to demand but then again takes the chance. Whether visible or concealed, demand itself does not result in realized consumption unless producers are willing to supply the product or service.

If the United States government wants to improve the economy, it needs to begin a systematic reduction of government programs and regulation. The federal government needs to give up on trying using fiscal policy to micro-manage the economy. Unlike Krugman, who sees a welfare state as an acceptable alternative, I see increasing government size as the very institution that perpetuates the need for a welfare state. Government needs to be seen for what it is: a necessary part of a market system where less is better and more begets more.

I don't see how people follow Marx but overlook his ultimate vision of a classless society where everyone produces according to their ability and receives according to their need. His vision was communism, and it has not worked very well. Those who believe in Keynesian economics have bought into government's ability to affect the economy in a positive way. But what about Keynes's prescription for the government to get out of the economy when things turned around? So-called mainstream economists have ignored this part of their philosophy.

Naivety of government's thirst for control has led the countries of Europe and around the world to high levels of unemployment, low productivity, and social unrest. To me, it is interesting to see how many command economy countries are moving away from socialism toward capitalism and free markets. It seems that the United States is rushing toward the government-controlled economy as quickly as others are rushing away from it. It seems to me that most of the people who believe government is the answer for an ailing economy or a failing market have never been in business for themselves or even worked for a company. I realize that this is a sweeping statement because there are a number of businessmen/politicians. If you want legislation that promotes business and prosperity, you probably should look at a business person rather than a career politician. The reasoning is that if you need swimming lessons, you will need someone who has a least strapped on a floaty.

6

How the U.S. government is perpetuating the demise of the American economy

This is not a Republican or Democratic issue. Unemployment, the credit crunch, the mortgage crisis, and corporate failures are all signs that the chickens are coming home to roost. You have to lie in the bed you made. Actions have consequences. It's time to pay the fiddler. We reap what we sow.

The good news is that there is a way out. Perhaps you ask, "Economic Comic, if we just don't continue to look for government to solve our problems, will that do it?" No. It is past that point. It is going to take a courageous and ferocious battle of the mind and body.

The founding fathers knew that government could not help but become a power grab. They had witnessed it firsthand. So they came up with a system that specifically, unequivocally stated that federal government shall not have any right not specifically granted in the Constitution. But using the interstate commerce clause to perpetuate funding blackmail and coercion, the federal government has spread like a kudzu vine swallowing up a forest until the trees can't see the light of day. For those of you that may not know, the planting of Kudzu was widely promoted government agricultural agencies in the 1930s–40s. Today, kudzu is referred to by the Oregon Department of Agriculture as a serious noxious weed and as an infestation that costs 500 million dollars annually in lost crop land and control measures. Government seems remarkably like the kudzu plant as described by experts. For the record, there are several uses for kudzu in terms of soil retention, feed for livestock, and various medical uses. But according to the Alabama Cooperative Extension Service, the fast growing plant becomes less usable over time and almost impossible to eradicate. *Science Daily* reports that kudzu is taking over 150,000 acres per year and has disastrous environmental consequences. Hmm, let's see. Kudzu was introduced by government agencies because it has some legitimate uses. But once planted it seems to expand at an uncontrolled pace, costing us lots of money, smothering growth of other plants. Livestock likes the initial kudzu leaves because they are so tasty, but in a short period of time the vines produce less and less and no longer produce anything of use. Suffocating and burdensome, the federal bureaucracy accounts for better than one-fifth of the entire U.S. gross domestic product. If you add in all government you can raise that figure to around forty percent. What a great analogy, Kudzu and the federal government!

Today, people are cutting back on purchases. Just what an inflationary economy ordered. Cutbacks on demand will at least keep prices in check, unless, of course, you have Uncle Sam (Bush 43) who decides to send you a stimulus check to artificially create demand. Right out of the Keynesian playbook. John Maynard Keynes blamed the 1930s' poor economy on lack of consumer spending. Paraphrasing in my best Yosemite Sam voice, "Too much saving goin' on here. Gov'ment needs to jump in there and give it some economic Viagra! Can't get it up on its own, you see!" Keynes theorized that even if government had to go into debt, the economy will only recover if the government plays the role of healer. Folks, if you believe in Keynesian economics, which evidently Bush 43 (and most administrations since 1932) did wholeheartedly, I must tell you again that Keynes also said that when the economy was going well, government should shut down programs, get out of the economy, and pay off debt.

In my most generous appraisal, Keynesian economics has been disfigured by the constant expansion of the federal government. But I see his basic reasoning as flawed, the same way the Karl Marx's and Robert Malthus's theories were flawed. Keynes just assumes that everybody that loses their job must just go home and wait for some to provide them with another. Marx saw power and wealth being concentrated in fewer and fewer hands. One could make the argument that is happening in the U.S. today! Not because of the free market but because of restrictions on free enterprise, complicated tax laws, and massive expansions of the money supply. If Robert Malthus was right, we would be starving and suffering from disease in most every part of the United States today. Instead, less than 5 percent of our population produces food in excess of our needs. Keynes contended that the economy could operate "on track" or just as easily spiral downward uncontrollably. Keynes focused on unemployment as a perpetuating problem rather than entrepreneurship as the natural reaction of the market. Marx and Malthus overlooked this potential for resourcefulness and innovation in their theories as well. In reality, during this downturn, if the government were market-driven, it would be cutting its spending too. Taxes and restrictions on businesses would be parried down, and any government programs that had grown in excess, or outlived its purpose, would be trimmed or eliminated to reduce spending.

Instead, the federal government has borrowed over ten trillion dollars. It portrays a tax cut as a cost. It pretends that a cut in government growth is a reduction in government. It is bailing out companies that should have been left to go out of business. It is giving tax credits for buying homes and trading in paid up cars. This simply encourages more debt and prolongs the price corrections that are needed in the market. The federal government started off to correct a broken finger; and sixty years later, we have a body cast that is a quarter of our weight. Stated less politely, the federal government is a cancer that feeds off our vital systems. For a man of my size, that is a forty-two-pound tumor that is causing my heart to work harder and harder to support all my vital functions. The economy needs chemotherapy and radiation. (I apologize in advance for those that have gone through this ordeal, including my wife.) It is not pleasant. We may still be able to survive. What we don't need is more of a government that caused the problem in the first place.

Paraphrasing the United States Constitution, the federal government is not allowed to do anything that is not expressly provided for in the Constitution.[27] That means that the Department of Education, Department of Human Health and Services, the EPA, and all other agencies have no right (it is illegal) to tell states how things must be done. As it is today, many states would be much better off as a separate country than a part of the

---

27 The Tenth Amendment limits the national government's powers to those expressly listed in the Constitution; the states, unless otherwise restricted, possess all the remaining (or "residual") powers of government.

United States. For example, for every dollar that New Jersey citizens pay in to the federal government, they receive about sixty-five cents in return. To get the money back, every state has to abide by the rules that the federal government lays down. Let me get this straight. I send money to someone who keeps 35 percent, out of which he takes a cut for himself and gives the remainder to someone else and then tells me what I have to do to get 65 percent of my money back. Now that makes sense!

Further, government has an inflationary impact on the economy, stifles business, causes shortages, and endangers the free markets. If one of government's goals over the past five decades has been to redistribute income from the upper class to the lower classes, it has failed to accomplish its goal. It has succeeded in doing just the opposite.

Government programs and regulations squeeze small business with restrictions and laws, making it so that only the legally robust corporations can prosper in the long run. Protection from big, bad business has always been a rallying cry of the activist, calling for additional government regulation and programs. Even with the onerous requirements of having employees and competing in the heavily regulated marketplace, seventy percent of businesses are sole proprietorships. Small business makes up in profit what it does not represent in sales volumes. When you look at corporate sales, it is about 80 percent of the total, and yet corporations write off enough of that money to only make 3 percent on the average as a return. Corporations report about 14 percent of the total income compared to about 9 percent for sole proprietorships (McConnell and Brue, 2007). Our laws allow for corporations to write off those huge salaries and "business expenses." Government regulation favors those who have experts that know how to exploit the law. Small business does not have the deep pockets to fend off lawsuits or buy corporate jets for that matter.

Corporations, with the government's taxing structure and liability laws, have shifted the advantage to big business. Marx predicted that capitalism would fail because big business would accumulate the power to exploit workers. The federal government has, unwittingly or not, been complicit with creating an environment that helped to usher in the very scenario that Marx claimed would happen.

7

National debt—biggest threat!

The national debt is a national disgrace. It makes us weak as a nation and invites others to consider attacking us. A first-week proclamation that the Obama budget would be balanced by the end of his first term got me all excited. Woo hoo! Somehow, the budget proposed triple of what Bush 43 signed. Oh my goodness. Are you serious? There is only one way out of this, and that is an across the board, systematic reduction of the federal government—no exceptions, no growth in any programs, an all-out freeze on any new spending. Our Constitution was trying to protect us from the very situation that we have today: an all-encompassing behemoth that grows on its own, as long as we sit by and don't say anything. The wealthy aren't complaining because they have learned to feast on the government's pork. The impoverished have become dependent on government and can only complain that they deserve more.

Texas Congressman Ron Paul has been sounding the warning bell for quite some time but has faced an uphill battle against an ingrained federal bureaucracy. Most anyone who tries to point out the unconstitutional nature of current government activities has been drowned out quickly or marked as a "crazy." The best way to get out of a hole is to stop digging. I don't who said this, but maybe President Obama will take notice, but the odds aren't good.

How can we ever live without all the government programs? Here's a great example. In 1977, the federal government created the Department of Energy. The government agency's stated goal was to lessen the U.S. dependence on foreign oil. Well, that has gone well. Thirty-two years later, a 24 billion-dollar budget, sixteen thousand federal employees, and a hundred thousand plus contract employees[28] have produced our current predicament. In thirty years since the inception of the Department of Energy, have we become less dependent on foreign oil? What's wrong with this picture?

All existing laws should be amended with an across the board sunset clause, with every government agency implementing a zero-based budget. It will be as painful as a family that is facing bankruptcy, having to sell all their possessions, and moving into a middle-class house. It is embarrassing that it has happened; but the sooner it is acknowledged, the more likely our country will survive. The Chinese have loaned us about $739 billion dollars and the Japanese $634 billion.[29] I guess the joke's on them if the U.S. securities are worthless. Boy are they going to be pissed when the U.S. sends them GM or AIG as payment. The Chinese evidently do not see the humor. But be warned by the saying, the man whose bread we eat is whose song we sing. In fact, they are already voicing their displeasure at our mismanagement of the dollar. But hey, we will just tell them that we need a bailout because we are too big to fail.

What will it take to get out of this mess? It will take a dynamic personality to raise the conscious level high enough to cause a groundswell of support for reducing the

---

28 http://www.energy.gov/energyefficiency/index.htm

29 http://www.uscc.gov/hearings/2007hearings/written_testimonies/07_05_24_25 wrts/07_05_24_2 5_setser_statement.pdf

federal government. We can hope that it does not require a complete financial collapse. There may have to be some stealth involved. To successfully reclaim our country will take a sneak attack. We must start electing closet fiscal conservatives to office. Then once in office, the disguise comes off and the person insists that every bill be part of a balanced budget and contain a sunset clause (sort of the opposite of Bush 41 and Bush 43)! Sneak attack! Say it again, Mufasa, sneak attack! I get excited just thinking about the possibility! The phasing out of government programs will create a landslide of resistance from those who have become addicted to power and money. It would take a special people indeed—patriots for sure—to withstand the hypocrites looking for their next sweet. The liberals who are quite comfortable with holding power over the poor and dependent will cry foul. The wealthy who are used to getting their pockets filled with nice government contracts will bellow. And when the wealthy and the elite left have a common interest, look out! This calls for a president with an *S* on his chest and an armor-protected plate on his back. It will take a patriot of the purest style.

Conclusion

I wrote this book as a means to express my frustration in a humorous way. I started out thinking that *What a Fine Mess* would be a rib tickler. Obvious to most, humor is a great way to get your point across. However, the more I wrote, the less humor I saw in the whole situation. I was momentarily encouraged when President Obama said that he would have a balanced budget by the last year of his term. That hope was quickly dashed when the latest budget roughly tripled that of what Bush 43 signed into law. I was briefly encouraged when Obama said that we should not expect government to solve all the problems that we face. That bit of sunshine has also been snuffed out with the current talk about the sweeping new programs that will be proposed. Our federal government is the source of the current calamity. Our ability to see our way through this crisis will come on the back of small business and the hard work of the middle and lower classes.

I was inspired by Samuel Adams, who said, "It does not take a majority to win, but rather an irate, tired minority that are willing to set the fires in people's minds."

Our system has served us well, despite our recent troubles. However, the US's past success does not mean continued good fortune. We, as a populace, need to begin promoting candidates who will systematically scale back government over time. We need selfless leaders who understand that the federal government should be a minimalist operation with a bias toward doing less. We need the balanced budget amendment that we were so close to having during Clinton's term. Clinton said, "See we can be fiscally responsible. We don't need a balanced budget amendment." We need fiscally conservative leaders with the backbone to withstand the barrage of hate rhetoric that will follow.

The day that politics became a vocation may have been the beginning of the end. We need an amendment that limits the terms of U.S. congressmen and senators. It won't be easy because, as Bob Ingles of South Carolina says, "Asking an incumbent member of Congress to vote for term limits is a bit like asking a chicken to vote for Colonel Sanders." So we, the citizens of the United States, will need a grassroots effort to force Congress to pass term limits.

We need to abolish the current income tax in favor of a consumption tax. Basic economics tells us that the income tax is the least desirable way to tax. It discourages activity that you want more of and rewards people for not complying. It is a game that has cost us billions of hours just to comply. The system has become onerous, and the IRS operates based on fear and intimidation. Our tax code is ludicrous. People are forced to sign their name to a coerced document. And somehow, in the land of civil rights and the likes of the ACLU, no one sees that as a violation.

The corporate tax system is out of whack. Eighty-four percent of revenue is generated from corporations.

When it comes to profit, that figure drops to 14 percent. Corporate leaders are not stupid. They collect as much revenue as they can and show as little profit as possible. Don't you do the same thing? You just don't have a high priced accountant to help you be as creative. This outcome is only possible because of a complex tax code. The federal government has created a complex system that only high-priced attorneys and accountants can exploit. If the federal government began taxing revenue instead of profits, not only would it create a fairer business climate but it would also create a whole new generation of leaner, more productive businesses.

This is not a case of seeking a government solution to solve a market problem. This is a solution to a market distortion created by government interference. Just as the case with environmental protection, we have witnessed public projects that destroy ecosystems instead of protecting them. The federal government's good intentions have led to horrendous and very painful unintended consequences of the economic and personal nature. You can take the war on drugs or the war on poverty or whatever the federal government tries to do; it is going to be, at best, inefficient. More than likely, the government will exacerbate the problem the legislation intended to correct and will cause harm in some other area. Our income distribution has become more disparate ever since the robust middle class of the 1960s began to dwindle. The war on poverty has resulted in a U.S. distribution of income that resembles a third-world nation (Johnston, 2008). And the battle cry for all the socialist movers and shakers is, "We need more government intervention to correct this huge problem."

We do have a problem, and it deserves repeating: when the barn is burning, don't ask the arsonist how to put out the fire. His answer will be more matches. The answer of more government simply makes the situation grow even more unstable. Government's poverty incentives, federal contracts, expansion of the money supply, national debt, and burdensome regulation are at the heart of it. A complicated tax system, entitlement programs, inflation, and special interest projects have perpetuated the "rich get richer" scenario. Meanwhile, the middle class gets shaken down and receives nothing; the welfare class produces little and is encouraged to wait for handouts; and the upper class sends in lots of income taxes, knowing that interest and contracts return money on the backside. This equation has not been so abhorrent as to call attention to itself, but baby it is a mean and nasty Doberman barking on our front porch now. Our purchasing power has continually dropped, and people have used debt to stay even or expand their standard of living. The middle class is getting the squeeze, and no phantom tax cut can make up for the fact that government spending continues to be a drag (and possibly the death nail) to the economy. What has caused the demise of the majority of nations during the course of history? My answer, but in the infamous words of the "scholar" Bill Clinton: "It is the economy, stupid." An Arkansas yuk yuk follows.

So I invite you to take up the banner of a fiscal conservative; proudly proclaim that you believe in limited government, balanced budgets, and free markets. Say that you understand that government is inherently inefficient and should be systematically reduced. Pledge not to look for government to solve our problems because you know that dispatching government will make the problem worse. Say aloud, in unison, "Government is a fan and a referee but not an owner or a player." Oh yes, I am feeling like the Economic Comic again, hopeful, optimistic, and proud of our country. Way to go, you fiscal conservative you!

References

BEA-Bureau of Economic Analysis (2008). Retrieved from bea.gov/national/nipaweb/TableView.asp?LastYear=2008

BEA-Bureau of Labor Statistics Web site, (2009). http://www.bea.gov/national/nipawcb/TableView.asp?SelectedTable=14&Freq=Qtr&FirstYear=2006&LastYear=2008

BLS-Bureau of Labor Statistics Web site, (2009). Retrieved from http://bls.gov.

Fulghum, R. (1998). *All I Really Need to Know I Learned in Kindergarten*. Toronto, Canada: Random House Publishing.

Gilder, G. (2003). *Wealth and Poverty*. San Francisco: ICS Publishing.

Irvine, J. (2002). *Talk About Sex*. California: Regent University.

Johnston, D. (2007). *Free Lunch*. New York: Penguin Group.

Krugman, P. (1999). *Accidental Theorist*. New York: W.W. Norton.

Levine, J. (2002). *Harmful to Minors: The Peril of Protecting Children.* University of Minnesota Press.

Perez, V. (2002) "Teenage Pregnancy: A Historical Legislative Analysis." http://wrt-intertext.syr.edu/X/contributors.html#VP.

Suskind, R. (2006). *The One Percent Doctrine.* New York: Simon and Schuster.

Tanner, M. (1995). "Congressional Testimony before Senate Judiciary Committee." 07–07–1995. Retrieve from http://www.cato.org/pubs/pas/pa-212.html

Updike, J. (2007). Retrieved from fhttp://www.newyorker.com/arts/critics/books/2007/07/02/070702crbo_books_updike?currentPage=3.

USOPM-United States Office of Personnel Management, (2009). Retrieved from http://www.opm.gov/.

⊖|LIVE

listen|imagine|view|experience

AUDIO BOOK DOWNLOAD INCLUDED WITH THIS BOOK!

In your hands you hold a complete digital entertainment package. In addition to the paper version, you receive a free download of the audio version of this book. Simply use the code listed below when visiting our website. Once downloaded to your computer, you can listen to the book through your computer's speakers, burn it to an audio CD or save the file to your portable music device (such as Apple's popular iPod) and listen on the go!

How to get your free audio book digital download:

1. Visit www.tatepublishing.com and click on the e|LIVE logo on the home page.
2. Enter the following coupon code:
   8813-299b-b709-2fdc-88c4-a46a-f44c-8fcf
3. Download the audio book from your e|LIVE digital locker and begin enjoying your new digital entertainment package today!